THE SEARCH FOR Grace

HEAL YOUR LIFE FROM THE INSIDE OUT

Krista Emma Gawronski

The Search for Grace
Heal Your Life From the Inside Out

Transcendent Publishing
www.TranscendentPublishing.com

TRANSCENDENT

ISBN: 979-8-9900956-8-7

Book Design: Shanda Trofe
Editor: Mary Rembert
Photographer: Faith Waitt

Printed in the United States of America.

Discover Grace

Dedication

I would like to dedicate this book to two amazing women in my life who have shaped my heart, beliefs, and character. This is for you, Mama. Thank you for your sacrifices to bring the most important values to our home, *Faith & Family.* And this is for my mother-in-law, Catherine, who taught me all about *Free Will & Grace.*

Contents

Foreword

I first met Krista at an event where I was co-facilitating with the phenomenal Sunny Dawn Johnston.

If you know Krista, you know that there's a type of other-worldly light that radiates from within and around her always. Her caring and supportive presence can instantly be felt within the first few seconds of being around her.

One of the things that stood out to me about Krista is her passion to be of service and how she can bring people together from all walks of life with such ease.

Krista walks through life with an open heart and is authentic with everything that she says and does. She is a natural leader, as extraordinary wisdom and guidance naturally flow through her as a speaker, teacher, and writer.

The words and guidance in this book will support you, the reader, with moving beyond deeply rooted traumas and struggles because Krista creates a safe and loving space for you to heal and thrive.

I am so grateful to witness Krista share her gifts and presence with the world, and I will be cheering her on every step of the way as she continues to help so many more.

With Joy,
Emmanuel Dagher
Spiritual Teacher, Speaker, Bestselling Author, & Founder of The Core Work Method
emmanueldagher.com

Gratitude

After I released my second book, ***Be Good, The Heart Centered Journey,*** I immediately began daydreaming about what my next writing project would be. I went into deep thought and considered ways of expanding myself as a person and a writer.

"How can I go deeper in my understanding of life?"

"How can I reach more people?"

"How can I spread the message of love in a world that has lost track of its priorities?"

I left the answers to those questions blank for a while. Subconsciously, I knew I would be guided to a divine path. I also had an inner knowing that any message worthwhile of my time and research would also require me to peel back layers of my story and do more work on myself.

It wasn't until I was invited to join a program called ***"The Sonoma Community Resilience Collaborative"*** that I knew which direction to take with my writing.[1] The program was installed to support people who suffered devastating losses from the Sonoma County fires. Community organizers collaborated with ***"The Center of Mind-Body Medicine"*** to teach an evidence-based curriculum for healing emotional trauma.

As fate would have it, I became a student of this grassroots program, and I learned from the founder, Dr. James Gordon. The

---

1 https://srhealth.org/collaborative/

mission of the work is to help communities around the world develop the tools they need to heal population-wide psychological trauma and stress. This program has assisted people who are dealing with anxiety, chronic pain, aging, grief, and life-threatening illnesses. It has helped people recover from the aftermath of war, tragedies, natural disasters, and devastating events.

Dr. Gordon's approach to healing is universal. It serves everyone regardless of age or educational level. He believes that we all have an untapped capacity to help and heal ourselves, which ultimately improves society as a whole. His professional background as a Psychiatrist, Clinical Professor at Georgetown University Medical School, and Chairman of the White House Commission on Complementary and Alternative Medicine Policy have provided him with the experience to lead this movement in healing and change the entire conversation around wellness and healthcare.

He has authored the book *Transforming Trauma: The Path to Hope and Healing.* This book gives a wonderful explanation of the stress response and how we can calm the nervous system down and shift fear and anxiety in the mind and body. The book is so informative as it highlights 50 years of Dr. Gordon's clinical experience and life-changing moments in which people discover their resilience and capacity to self-heal.

As a practitioner, I'm empowered to facilitate mind-body medicine groups and teach everyday people self-care tools to address their emotional healing. This program has taken me to another level of leadership and freedom within myself. I now have a better understanding of how trauma and unexpressed emotions can affect our physical health, self-confidence, immune system, mental health, spiritual well-being, relationships, and life decisions. Everything is connected to the inner self.

I would like to thank Dr. Gordon for his groundbreaking role in wellness. The skills offered through this program are not only supportive of a person's physical health, but they reinforce compassion and self-awareness. Dr. Gordon's commitment to humanity has paved the way for us to improve our operations in healthcare, mental health, and social work and meet the emotional needs of our fellow human beings.[2]

I feel very honored to facilitate groups and elevate the world's understanding of personal healing. This modality reinforces the importance of self-care and managing emotions. We are invited to understand the relationship between loss and love ... pain and purpose. Once we take the journey inward, we shall see that we can hold space for both energies and expand our wisdom. This is the nature of the human condition. All experiences are taking us further along in our resilience and spiritual transformation.

I would also like to acknowledge Jerrol Kimmel, RN, MA,[3] and Tanmeet Sethi, MD, Integrative and Psychedelic Medicine, and author of *Joy Is My Justice.*[4] These two women have worked alongside Dr. Gordon and were instrumental in my training. They demonstrated confidence and kindness. They were so intuitive and encouraging. They showed me the power of a circle and how listening can help a person shift their pain. Their examples of Grace gave me a bar of excellence to follow.

There are a number of spiritual teachers and mentors who have provided education and support to me over the last ten years, and each has had divine timing in my growth and purpose.

2 https://cmbm.org/team/team-member/james-gordon/
3 https://cmbm.org/team/team-member/jerrol-kimmel/
4 https://www.tanmeetsethimd.com/

Thank you to Sunny Dawn Johnston for her lessons in self-care and spirituality.[5] She has been an amazing teacher in my life and has taught me valuable lessons in self-love. I've taken her certification programs in Mind-Body Spirituality and Reiki. Sunny introduced me to archangels and taught me to tap into my psychic skills. As a result, I've become a much more intuitive leader, teacher, speaker, and writer. She's helped me see myself through a lens of wholeness and unconditional love, and I'm forever grateful. Best of all, I consider her a dear friend.

I want to thank Liz Dawn, who has been a fearless leader in bringing spiritual conversations to the forefront with *"Celebrate Your Life."*[6] She created one of the best platforms for authors and spiritual teachers to share their message of self-love and peace. I took her speaker training several times and learned to be comfortable with myself and passionate about my message. Liz loves to laugh, tell good stories, and talk about ways to make the world better. There's something about her drive to have fun, put on high-caliber events, and help others see their inner light that mirrors my own passion and vision for the world. I'm grateful for her example.

I have deep gratitude for Emmanuel Dagher for giving me a beautiful perspective on teaching spirituality and healing.[7] His gentle message of self-acceptance gave me permission to see myself with Grace and possibility. I spent my 49th birthday at a retreat with Emmanuel and Sunny in Sedona, and something within me "woke up." I realized that I was playing life small. I left that retreat very excited about my path in writing and teaching and stopped imposing fear and restrictions on myself.

---

5 https://sunnydawnjohnston.com/
6 https://celebrateyourlife.com/events/
7 https://emmanueldagher.com/

Emmanuel has an incredible life story. His mission to facilitate peace and healing began long ago. He grew up in the war-torn country of Lebanon. The traumas of war sparked a higher calling for his life to bring forward light and consciousness to others. His compositions in music and meditations and his genius work in "*The Core Work Method*" have made him a transformation specialist. Emmanuel has had the honor of presenting at the United Nations and the World Congress, as well as other national and international events and summits that promote peace and healing. It's a joy to call him a friend and have his presence in my book. The three most powerful words that Emmanuel taught me were, "I see you."

Books don't come together on their own. If you want to have amazing exposure and traction, you really need someone who knows the ins and outs of the publishing field. For me, that is Shanda Trofe of *"Transcendent Publishing."* [8] I am deeply appreciative of her guidance over the years. She's at the top of her craft. This book marks our third collaboration. Shanda introduced me to a wonderful circle of spiritual teachers, healers, and leaders, which changed the trajectory of my life. Of course, our shared love for Kid Rock makes us the ideal team. I want to thank her for her encouragement when things weren't happening fast enough. She told me, "Be patient. This book will be birthed when it's ready." She was right.

Family … It's one of the most important things in my life. Paul has been my rock and has been supportive of my writing. Even if he didn't always understand that inspiration comes at 4 a.m., he's always cheered me on. I love how he's trusted me to listen to my inner voice. He's encouraged me to do what I need to fulfill my spiritual purpose. I don't think he's ever really known how much it's meant to have him wake up every morning at 7:30 a.m., start

---

8 https://www.transcendentpublishing.com/

the coffee, and say, "Good Morning, Sunshine. Are you winning?"

It goes without saying just how much I love my two sons. Frank and Vince have been a big part of my inspiration for writing this book. It's been my desire as a mother to provide them with a deeper understanding of life and the importance of being in touch with their emotions and spirituality. Every decision they ponder can be resolved by their courage to go inward. It makes no difference what the question is. The answer is always *LOVE!*

I want you both to know just how proud I am to be your mother. I admire your love of God, country, and family. If you listen to your spiritual guidance and follow your heart, you will have the most fulfilling life, be engaged in a higher purpose, and attract the most extraordinary people. Wherever I am, I'm cheering you on. I'm still that mom in the grandstands with a cowbell and a proud smile.

My family has inspired me greatly throughout this process. They've had a huge role in my growth over the years. My faith is so strong because of my mother, Gail. She has made tremendous sacrifices for our family. She instilled the value of family in all of us and taught us about spiritual dedication. She has always understood my need to fly on my own, even though I was the last one to leave the nest. I've appreciated her trust in my gifts and dreams. My father, Armando, instilled curiosity in me at a very young age, and he taught my family to stand up for what we believe in. This book holds the gentle parts of him and his powerful wisdom.

My brothers have always wanted the best for me. I love you, Robert, Artie, and Armando. I hope this book reminds you of how resilient and deserving you are. My sisters, Sylvia and Sandy, have always been my greatest cheerleaders *(three girls in a little pink room).* Thank you for your unconditional love. You have been powerful examples in my life. I love you more than you know. There's nothing stronger than the bond of sisterhood.

I'm also grateful to my larger support system: Mark, Ron, Angie, Tory, Ali, Danny, Joni, and Jenny. Thank you to my aunties, uncles, cousins, nieces, nephews, and beautiful sister friends from Sonoma County and Anthem, who have encouraged me to follow my dreams. Some part of each of you is in this book.

Nothing happens by chance. I want to thank Faith Waitt for stepping in to take my photos for my book and website.[9] It seemed fitting to be at *"The Little White Church."* You captured the "Real Me," and I'm grateful I discovered your amazing gifts.

My heartfelt appreciation goes to: Lynn Kohler, Erin and Karen, Lisa Baird, Wendi Thomas, Melissa Becker, Paula Obeid, Julie Chacon, Jewelee Tompulis, Stef and Paula, my Birthday Tribe, and Sturgis Girls for that extra encouragement to cross the finish line.

Warm thanks to Mary-Beth Ray for your delightful support over the years with design projects and bookmarks. You make everything homemade with love.

Thank you to my editor, Mary Rembert, who stepped in at the perfect time to bring flow and ease to every chapter.

My sincere gratitude goes to Peach for all the work that we did together in our mind-body medicine journey. We grew so much. I now know that you never go anywhere without your beautiful heart (LOL)! The work in this book represents years of collaborative study, workshops, and brave inner work. Thank you for

---

9 https://faithvalega.shootproof.com

coining the phrase, "Whole, Creative, and Resourceful." There's nobody like you!

I want to thank my father-in-law for his unconditional love and support. Because of his sacrifices, we are in a position to do the things we love and serve others. Lastly, I want to thank Cathy, my mother-in-law. She and I "got each other." She told me that I was one of her best friends, which is still one of the greatest honors of my life. She was The Italian Princess, The Golden Girl, The Wise Matriarch, The Proud Conservative, The Beautiful Dragonfly, and The Messenger of Love and Joy. May we all live as graciously as she did.

Special Note From the Author

Thanks for allowing me to express my gratitude to those who have supported me in my journey.

The Search for Grace has been one of the most rewarding and challenging experiences of my life. I know deep within my heart there is something special in this book waiting to be unwrapped by you. This book holds the best wisdom that I've learned over time from life experiences, loved ones, teachers, and healers. It's fitting that some of the greatest lessons I've learned surfaced during times of grief and adversity.

We cannot begin to know the value of experiences until we sit with our emotions. There are infinite ways to do this and relieve yourself of stress or conflict. I won't tell you that my approach to healing is *"the right way"* or even *"the only way"* to navigate stressful changes, but I promise to walk you through a gentle process that will help you feel lighter. It will empower you in surprising ways.

Before we start, I have just one recommendation … **stay open**. You never know how new perspectives or the exercises in this book can improve your health, free your mind of worry, or uplift your spirit. Each chapter has the potential to wake up some part of yourself that has been dormant, or it could inspire healthy habits, ignite your passion, or spark new creativity.

Your life is a wonderful love story in the making. I hope you see yourself as the leading role in your peace, wellness, and happiness. When you acknowledge yourself as your own healer, no person, situation, or extraneous noise can disrupt that love for yourself or hold you back from fulfilling a dream. My heart tells me that by making space for Grace, you shall experience more joy and miracles. I want that for you.

I did something different with this book. I've incorporated questions, meditations, and exercises to add to your experience. Feel free to go at your own pace. While these will be optional, you have an opportunity to connect with yourself on a deeper level. You can examine your own beliefs, spirituality, and capacity to heal. The tools and journal exercises will give you a supportive framework for introspection. Of course, the more you pour your heart into this process, the more benefits you will receive.

All of the questions in this book are designed to help you get to know yourself more intimately and get in touch with your full self … your magical child, your traumas, your survival behaviors and defense mechanisms … your divine guidance, your dreamer, and your higher consciousness. Know that whatever intentions you have for healing, self-improvement, and spiritual growth are being realized at this moment by a power greater than yourself.

Love,

Krista

Chapter One

It's Going to Be Okay

W ell, I can't tell you just how excited I am to release this book to the world. It's tugged at my heart for the past several years. To be honest, there were moments when I wanted to just let the whole thing go, but every single time I set aside my laptop, God would call me back. I kept hearing, **"You can do this ... Keep going."**

Sometimes, I labored over chapters and other times, I spent days on just one paragraph, and I often wondered, "What is it all for?" Was this book just one more thing that I was putting pressure on myself to finish, or was there some greater reason for which it could serve others in their wellness journey? Well, one must be very careful of the questions they ask the Universe, for the answers could be very surprising.

Let me set the scene for what would become the inspiration for *The Search for Grace.* It was November 2020, and I was participating in an online writer's retreat. The world was in the middle of a Covid lockdown. Everyone was dealing with so much stress and fear, and people across the world needed some calming force. I began reflecting on my education in Mind-Body Medicine and Spirituality. I instinctively felt like this work could be a saving Grace for a lot of people who were struggling.

Covid reinforced separation, and it presented us with the strangest dilemmas. We didn't know how to be with other people comfortably, and we certainly didn't know how to be by ourselves either. The pandemic would reveal another level of human frailty, but it would also present the world with a tremendous opportunity to expand spiritually and elevate our consciousness.

My self-awareness grew tremendously during that time, and I learned something very important about the human spirit. Peace is largely determined by our willingness to address our emotions and fears. Covid shined a spotlight on our poor emotional habits and survival behaviors that reinforce chaos, separation, and disorder. I could see that there's a strange movement that is taking us further away from our true selves and spirituality.

We cannot neglect the inner self and expect to find a peaceful world. Everything is a microcosm of the way we love and take care of ourselves. Most people don't think about the relationship between their divinity and harmony in the world, but they are intertwined. Each person has an assignment on earth to bring forward their love and gifts to enhance, improve, inspire, or uplift the world in some small way.

We have stepped into this strange reality where the outer world has become more important than our inner peace. It's that disconnect that has caused many of us to neglect our emotions, physical maintenance, mental health, and spiritual well-being. This has changed our personal priorities and the way that the world operates. Everything is faster, people are stressed out, and we seem to be losing sight of the fundamental values that once united us. If you throw in politics, things get really fu#%ing weird.

We live in a world where stress and fear rule our behavior, and we're becoming desensitized to the larger social problems that affect our health and humanity. I'm guessing you picked up this book because this reality disturbs you as well, and you're asking yourself how you can live with more Grace and Ease. More importantly, how do we come together?

We cannot deny one simple fact: we are all in the same little boat and have taken on water. Our response cannot be about individual survival but our collective safety and well-being. There isn't a single problem that cannot be improved by love. When people say they are hopeless and powerless, my answer is to look inward. Nothing inspires a person better than spirituality and the sound of their heartbeat. Once we learn to calm the storm inside our bodies, we can restore balance in society.

Now, most people don't see themselves as part of a greater solution to humanity, and that complacency has created a shortage of love. This book affirms the importance of spiritual growth and reinforces your responsibility to every person in the boat. By committing to your healing and connecting with your spiritual priorities, you not only take ownership of your health and happiness, but you also raise the frequency of the positive energy flowing in the world.

Human behavior is a fascinating study. People may have a certain vision for their lives, and when things don't meet their expectations, emotional conflict sets in. Eventually, it will need to be addressed. If you can't honor your emotions, listen to your divine guidance, or affirm self-love, you shall post your search outside yourself. You'll hustle for the validation and love that you cannot give to yourself or latch onto some temporary fix that makes you feel better. This sets up a series of habits and behaviors that contradict inner peace.

Life becomes a fruitless experience when we put other people in charge of our joy and peace. If you don't believe you can manage your well-being, that's when you suffer. So, what do I know about suffering? Well, it may surprise you just how much we all know. It is embedded into our human experience. To be able to sit quietly with ourselves and be with our emotions has to be one of the most difficult challenges in life, but it becomes the foundation for everything … our joy, our freedom, and our physical and emotional well-being.

When you don't feel comfortable being in your own skin, you build walls and set up emotional barriers that interfere with your confidence, creativity, relationships, and connection to your higher self. As a society, we aren't formally taught to manage our emotions or discomfort. Most of us are just winging it. However, the Universe will show us time and time again that no amount of distraction, denial, or avoidance can suppress the lessons intended for us.

Life has this push-and-pull dynamic. There will be times when you are drawing people, opportunities, lessons, and energy toward you … and then there are other times when you are called to release burdens, beliefs, and relationships that are interfering with your growth. We must remember that we own nothing, and so the most challenging part of healing is staying fluid … allowing positive and negative experiences to flow through us without attachment.

If you look around the planet, there are far too many people who are feeling stuck, stagnant, and consumed by fear because they haven't found a way to work **WITH** their emotions. The only way to know real freedom is to meet that resistance in your life and trust that it has something valuable to teach you. In trying to bypass pain, we have become a numb society, and so I have concluded that what the world is really calling for is more healing, self-compassion, and faith in something greater than ourselves.

It's time to replace our burdens, sickness, and fear with more GRACE and LOVE.

Sharing this work and giving people a kind approach to healing excites me. Most people go through life compartmentalizing their pain … picking and choosing when they can be real. It is a survival response that serves as temporary protection, but when we hide who we are and what we feel, we settle on a life that doesn't feel like our own anymore. For some reason, that is no longer okay for me. I've got to stay REAL!

I have learned that when we are brave enough to go inward and be with our emotions exactly as they are, we are bound to no one, and we are no longer a victim of our traumas. The freedom I refer to in this book is about being present and unafraid to stand in your raw, unfiltered story. It's the realization that love is possible at all times, even when you feel broken or helpless. While I have learned that it's not necessary to explain, solve, or rationalize pain, our greater responsibility to ourselves is to just listen to it.

For years, we have been conditioned to hide or demonize our emotions. Many people keep their pain, shame, fear, sadness, inadequacy, loneliness, disappointment, grief, and feelings of abandonment a secret. The tools and messages in this book will help you see the importance of honoring your emotions. Most of us feel limited because we carry beliefs that we aren't safe, capable, worthy, or supported, but that's just fear talking. This book offers a gentle path forward where you see yourself as spiritual and resilient.

And so it began. I found myself arranging the information for this book to meet a need in public health and address a spiritual void. My intention was to assist others in their journey to see themselves as resourceful and free themselves from stress, chaos, fear, and any tangled energy that holds them back from living each day to the fullest.

While that inspiration would prove meaningful, I found out later on that same retreat that there was also something more personal driving this book. I just needed a good teacher to pull it out of me. Sunny Dawn Johnston was one of the facilitators of my writer's retreat. She has been my spiritual teacher, business mentor, and friend for many years. I remember that exact moment when she asked the group, **"How many of you know your WHY for writing your book?"**

I raised my hand for a quick answer, "I want to help people." It was short and sweet. After all, how could anyone possibly argue with being helpful? I went on to share, **"I want to share my education around Mind-Body Medicine so that people can learn to deal with their emotions and address any underlying stress that affects their well-being."**

Sunny knew that the moment you arrive at the easy answer, there's usually more to it. She would push me further to confront my resistance. She directed another question my way, **"So why does that matter?"** I felt a little irritated at her, but I answered the best that I could, **"It matters because most of us weren't taught how to work with our emotions, and so we end up wasting a lot of time, tears, and energy trying to avoid the truth of who we really are."** She drew fire again and asked the same stupid question, **"And why does that matter?"**

I paused for a minute and felt the tears well up in the corner of my eyes. It made no difference that we were on a Zoom call. I felt like I was twelve in the front of the classroom, trying to figure out the answer to a ridiculous algebra question on the chalkboard. I absorbed all the uncomfortable silence. I looked at my laptop and saw seventeen faces staring at me and waiting for some meaning-ful answer. My lips quivered, and I eventually blurted out loud, **"Don't you get it? I needed this book for much of my life!"** My cheeks heated up, and I felt embarrassed about the outburst.

I quickly brought my volume down and explained, "There were so many times in my life when I needed to hear that I was going to be okay when things around me felt chaotic, scary, and uncer-tain. I wanted to feel better, but I didn't see myself as strong or worthy. I didn't have the tools to handle fear, disappointment, or grief, nor did I have the courage to tell anyone what I was feeling. I made a pact with that little girl to hide anything shitty or un-comfortable. Sadly, it took years to realize that I had lost a part of myself."

I thought about what I had just admitted. I was so embarrassed. I thought to myself, *How ironic! Here we were in the middle of a pandemic where people were wearing masks and hiding from a virus, and yet I had just come clean ... I had been wearing a mask for years.* I felt like I had just opened Pandora's box.

Sunny became soft and asked me a final question, "And why does that little girl still matter?" I looked at Sunny and spoke from a place of total vulnerability. "I have been self-critical for most of my life. I judged my feelings all the time and decided that my feelings were either 'GOOD' or 'BAD.' I put the bad ones in a little box, never to be found. I put pressure on myself to be per-fect, and when I didn't meet that expectation, I felt ashamed and unworthy. I suppose this book is for her, who needed permission to just be with her sadness, anger, and disappointment. She didn't trust that everything was going to be okay."

Everyone could feel my vulnerability, and the group remained quiet and watched. I saw some people wipe away their tears, and I knew that we had just peeled a big fucking onion. Something shifted for me in that moment as a person and as a writer. I had finally taken ownership of my story and really started to understand my need for Grace.

Regardless of all those good intentions to serve others, I now had a much more personal and compelling reason for pouring myself into this book. Sunny then addressed me in a kind voice, "Well, my friend, I think you now understand your TRUE WHY for writing this book."

That moment was a game changer because I realized that I not only had something powerful to teach, but I still had something important to heal in my own life, so I have now left space in my heart for both intentions. It's actually quite beautiful because it represents the circular exchange of giving. When we set out to elevate others, we ultimately heal something within ourselves that needs love.

This book has not only become a mission to support others on their journey but is a gift to my soul. I'm committed to replacing old survival patterns and releasing any shame or fear around expressing my feelings. To say that this work has freed me is an understatement. It has allowed me to release self-judgment and bring in self-compassion. I now know that our emotions are here to teach us about self-love and resilience, and every shitty thing that happens in life is just an invitation to get in touch with God or whatever divine spirit that fortifies you.

Whether you agree or disagree with this premise, many of us grew up without any language or tools for emotional healing. As you approach this book, know that the terms of human life are universal. We will all experience fear, disappointment, loss, and mortality, and we won't have control in how those experiences unfold. However, it becomes our choice and privilege to decide how we will respond to those moments.

It becomes vital to our health to listen to our bodies and honor our stories. Nobody can do that for us, and when you make that decision, you shall arrive at true peace and freedom. This is where your higher consciousness lives. I suppose there was a time when I thought that I needed someone to tell me that I would be okay, but what I now understand is that we find that wisdom by taking the long journey inward.

So here we are. We are neither broken nor alone. We are just transforming ourselves and learning to navigate through life with more Grace. Let us enter this journey from a position of strength and forward progress, for our resilience relies on the transformation of self in which we breathe in our wholeness and trust that every tangled experience we go through is just bringing us closer to God.

Stay Brave.

Love,

Krista

Personal Reflection/Setting Your Intention

For this exercise, you will need a comfortable chair, a pen, and something to write on. You may want to dedicate a new journal for your notes, revelations, and future exercises.

Take a moment for yourself right now. Go to a quiet place where there are no people, distractions, or loud noises. Find a comfortable chair to sit on. If your mind feels busy, take a few slow cleansing breaths in through the nose and out through the mouth. Do this as many times as you would like. Allow any sounds or sighs that want to come through. Everything is gentle and effortless.

With both feet flat on the floor, adjust your body to the chair so your back feels supported. If there is something that you can do right now to get more comfortable, feel free to modify your position. Once you are ready, place your right hand over your heart and rest your left hand over your belly. Breathe in and out slowly. Notice your hands moving up and down with every inhalation and exhalation. Take as many breaths as you need to settle in.

When you feel ready, pose this question out loud, **"What would you have me learn?"**

Feel free to repeat the question as many times as you need. An answer will eventually come. It might be one word, or it could be a sentence. There is no rush, and there are no wrong answers. This is an exercise that requires patience and self-kindness. If it is helpful, you may close your eyes and ask the question again. **"What would you have me learn?"** Continue this process until you arrive at an answer, and then you can write down any thoughts that come forward.

"What would you have me learn?"

Now, the beauty of this question is realizing that you are in a partnership with your higher spirit. Together, you shall arrive at an answer that supports your physical well-being, soul, and life as you currently know it. Stay open. Your first answer is typically the best and truest answer. There is no need to overthink this process or change anything to make it sound better. This is an exercise that is only for your eyes. Allow time and space for a message to come. This shall be your operating intention as you move forward in this book.

Should you reflect on this question further, you may decide to elaborate. Just know that the answer will always come from a place of Grace. That's right, we are already in touch with Grace. Everything that comes from this energy will be kind and supportive.

Chapter Two

The Unraveling

I believe that there are no coincidences. The fact that you and I are coming together right now is divine. You see, we are not only raising the frequency in one another but in the world as well. Every time we decide to invest in ourselves, we are essentially elevating the collective vibration. There has never been a more pressing time for us to take better care of our health, humanity, and the planet.

My intuition tells me that something inside of you is ready for change. How do I know that? Well, it's because it's simply not possible to keep up with the rest of the world in its present state. Intuitively, we all know that the pace is just way too fast, and the energy it requires comes at a tremendous cost to one's physical, mental, emotional, and spiritual well-being.

Not too long ago, I read an Indian proverb shared by English author Margaret Rumer Godden. It characterizes each human being as a "house." Within this house, there are four rooms that represent the physical, mental, emotional, and spiritual aspects of being human. The analogy sets up an interesting dilemma. As humans, we tend to live in one room most of the time. However, unless we are willing to go into every room every day, if only to keep it aired out, we will likely feel incomplete.

The fact that you are currently searching for Grace confirms that you are ready to pull back on the reins, explore all those other rooms, and get in tune with the things that matter to your heart. Now, that may seem difficult for the person who has been entrenched in lots of responsibilities or feeling the pressure to hold things together for everyone around them, but at some point, your needs must rise to the top. It's important to recognize that self-love is just as important as the energy you pour into your family, friendships, job, and community.

This reminds me of a conversation I once had with my father. He said, "Krista, everything is just smoke! You can't take any of it with you. One moment, something is here, and the next moment, it's gone ... people, material things, your job, what you perceive to be your identity ... the illusion of importance. At some point, you have to decide what's actually important to YOU, and it will fully contradict what the world tells you."

He didn't sugarcoat life, but that's okay because he was very much on point. He wanted me to stay real, and I suppose there was a time when I didn't even know what that meant for myself. It wasn't until I embarked on a journey of self-discovery that everything changed for the better because I started looking at life more objectively.

Most people start taking an inventory of their lives around their 40s. It's about the time that we all look in the mirror and see a person who has already experienced love and loss. Eventually, we must evaluate how those life experiences shape us. There's an internal wisdom that comes into play during our adulthood, where we shift our focus. Instead of thinking that life is happening to us, we realize that we are participants in our happiness.

During that period, we are likely to confront the harsh constructs of the world. We see human suffering all the time in the people who live on the streets, but what if I told you that the majority of the population are in their pretty homes quietly enduring their stress and hiding their grief? They wake up each day and put on their pain like a weighted vest. They get used to carrying it, and pretty soon, they no longer know what it's like to be light.

The truth is, you may not be able to identify the person who has chronic levels of pain or even see stress in yourself because we've all gotten very good at disguising our emotions, fears, and sadness. When you realize that critical life energy is tied to the way that you hold in your feelings, you can courageously instill changes to your life that support your mind, body, and spirit.

Whether pain takes on a physical problem, symptom, illness, dysfunctional behavior, or it just remains a quiet storm within, it is an invitation to do some soul-searching. Now, this is about the time that people typically shut down or turn away from their pain. It's certainly not because they don't want to feel better. It's because they are either scared to be with their feelings or they aren't sure they know how to process their grief or traumas.

When people can't find the strength or courage to meet their pain, they will find comfort elsewhere. Distractions could be work or social media pages. Maybe it's with another human being. Comfort is often found in food, alcohol, weed, vacations, shopping, etc. For people who don't want to deal with their emotions, those behaviors may provide some short-term relief, but they aren't long-term remedies. Pain waits for us.

I have learned that searching for Grace is not about arriving at a particular place or crossing some finish line. It is a never-ending process in which we give ourselves permission to be with the raw pieces of our story, feel our emotions, and administer self-compassion and forgiveness as needed. Grace grants us the courage and wisdom to get to the other side of pain, and believe it or not, love is always waiting for us.

This is the soul's journey, and it's not only happening in this lifetime but will continue well into the next realm when you shed the physical shell known as your body. When you are stuck in the trenches of sadness or conflict, Grace creates the space for healing. While most people are just searching for a way to get through the day, Grace takes away that painful feeling that you are enduring in your life.

Now, you may not have viewed Grace as some spiritual convergence, but that's exactly what it is. It is a deeply profound collaboration in which you and your higher power work together to restore peace and balance. My guess is this is where the phrase "By the Grace of God" came from. We not only find our courage to overcome hardships but also transmute the friction that holds us back in fear. We awaken to another level of consciousness in which we view ourselves and the world with unconditional love.

Have you ever thought to yourself, *Once I get through this shit, I'll be happy.* Well, Grace is what moves you through the storm. It's that mercy that only you can give to yourself. There are no generic terms that we can use to label pain. It's quite personal and subjective. It arrives in a nondescript package, and YOU have to open and release it.

There are infinite ways in which it shows up in our bodies and behavior, and the longer it is held or ignored, the more it perpetuates stress and feelings of bitterness and hopelessness. This is why so many of us are ready to loosen our grip on life. We are burned out, and our bodies are exhausted from trying to hold onto pain so tightly. We no longer have the bandwidth to carry problems that don't belong to us.

We are definitely ready to invite more peace into our lives. There's something inside all of us that needs a sanctuary … a safe place to express who we are. We need to feel grounded in an energy greater than ourselves and know that our presence in the world means something. Now, I suppose some people might see that as a place they go to physically, but I am suggesting that you connect with the tranquility already inside you.

Indulge me for a moment as we go back to the very beginning. Each human is born into this life with divinity. We embody an essence so pure and wholesome that it's easy to recognize the Grace and godliness within human life. In fact, it's not uncommon to hear people say, "Babies are such miracles." We hold them, love them, nurture them, and accept them. There is absolutely nothing that they have to do to prove their worth.

You cannot look at a newborn without feeling inspired. Think about how expressive and animated babies are. They don't overthink love or put restrictions on themselves. They are free-spirited beings, and what I mean by that is they move, make sounds, and respond to everything and everyone based on what they feel or need in the moment.

That free-flowing energy is innate. However, it changes once we start adapting to the rest of the world. We slowly take on more and more energy, pressure, rules, fear, and the expectations of society and authority figures. Of course, things are further complicated by technology and social media. However **"normal"** this entire passage is, socialization imposes some very tight restrictions on our spirit, and it tangles our energy constantly.

We become more inhibited over time because we feel the pressure to meet the expectations of others. When we start experiencing sadness, embarrassment, shame, abandonment, or disappointment, we begin losing something very precious—our innocence.

We often hold back who we really are or what we feel because we fear negative reactions, rejection, or social consequences.

Yes, life presents us with some rather interesting challenges where we must continuously question what is **REAL** and what is **SMOKE**. Not too long ago, I saw a funny meme being passed around on social media.

SOCIETY: "Be yourself."

SOCIETY: "No, not like that!"

While it's pretty humorous, it highlights the pressure that society places on each and every one of us. To adhere to all the physical, social, financial, and family demands, we have to lose a part of our true selves.

Take a moment to think about your early childhood and how it's ingrained in your belief system that being compliant is more important than being yourself. We are instructed at a very young age not to make waves or color outside the lines, and if we do what is expected of us, then there's a very good chance that we will be rewarded. This has made us excellent performers.

So, when does this conditioning take place? Well, our first glimpse of this reward system begins in the home with our family of origin. We quickly learn to be a good little girl/boy and follow directions. Later, we graduate to other social settings and authority figures—friends, teachers, coaches, employers, etc. Eventually, we settle into the larger world that is performance-driven, and there is compensation for what we do and what we look like instead of who we are.

Conditioning happens very early. Children are told not to speak out of turn, disappoint others, cry, or make a scene. We learn to hold in our feelings and tears, and pretty soon, that behavior crosses over into the way we communicate our thoughts and ideas, laugh out loud, express our talent and creativity, or even share our feelings or personal stories.

Instead of being in a higher state of consciousness, we become insecure and self-conscious. This is a developmental shift that all humans go through, and it changes the way we express our true selves in the world. As soon as we learn to say "Yes" or "No," another level of conditioning and authority kicks in. Pretty soon, speaking our truth, voicing our opinions, sharing our emotions, or expressing what we need can be met with resistance.

You can see it so clearly when you take yourself out of the equation. For instance, when a child says, "No, I don't want to do that …" a power struggle happens. A parent might have any of these reactions:

"Now, that's not how you talk to Mommy. **You need to say that you are sorry right now!**"

"It doesn't matter if you don't want to. **You will do what you are told!**"

"I'm very *disappointed* in you!"

"You're being very *bad* right now!"

"If you don't listen, there will be *NO* dessert tonight!"

"You have made me very upset. **Go to your room!**"

We can identify with all of these situations, and what I would like for you to consider is how a child's early experience of speaking their truth may subconsciously carry over into adulthood. If speaking up is associated with judgment, disapproval, punishment, or separation, a person is more likely to hold back their truth, ideas, and feelings. Now, that may not have been the intention at the moment, but fear changes our natural behavior.

I'm curious how freedom would serve you today. What would it be like to express your full self without any resistance or fear? At our age, it is more important to be authentic than compliant. We not only have our base values, but we can determine better than anyone else what is truly in our best interest. You might say that we are in a critical position right now to dismantle some of those old beliefs and conditionings that no longer serve us. After all, now that we are older and wiser, we understand that it's possible to say "No" politely.

It's a wonder how we begin our journey with so much light and openness, and then we take on the density of the world. We catch our breath, contract our bodies, swallow our words, postpone our joy, and hold back parts of ourselves, all in the name of pleasing others and fitting in. Strangely, those are the very same behaviors that have also made us sick, depressed, and unhappy.

Our younger selves saw each day as a blank canvas—an adventure of the heart. There are times when I think about my younger self, and I miss her. If I close my eyes, I can see her long, stringy brown hair and freckles. I love that she wore clothes that didn't match. She was so present and saw wondrous things in people and nature. She painted, climbed trees, and roller-skated for hours.

That little girl was in touch with her freedom and God. She would get lost in her dreams and imagination. She didn't carry words like **"CAN'T or DON'T."** She danced to the songs that played in her mind. She twirled and skipped and looked at life with complete joy and wonder.

Now, I'll be honest: it's been rather eye-opening to spend time thinking about this little girl who is still inside me. It wasn't until I started this introspective journey that I understood that Grace unfolds once we make space for that child within. That is where we are uninhibited, and we can experience the strong presence of God.

Perhaps what has been lost in translation over time is that there is an unconditional aspect of God's love. It doesn't waiver in times of adversity or personal frailty, but it's important to recognize that our connection with God flourishes or suffers based on how we treat ourselves. Within every situation that we buy into the conditioning, the noise, or the beliefs that we aren't good enough, strong enough, or worthy enough, we not only turn away from everything that is sacred, magical, and resilient about ourselves but we put up barriers between ourselves and God.

I find it rather interesting that when bad things happen to us or in the world, our first question is, **"Well, where the hell is God?"** What I hope to do in this book is change that knee-jerk response to a different question, **"Where am I right now? Is fear dominating this experience, and how have I strayed from my true self and spirituality?"** That shift in mentality is so important because it allows you to see yourself as more of a participant in your life and less of a victim.

We are driving this human experience. Our health, fulfillment, and happiness are highly determined by our investment of love and energy in ourselves. Whether we recognize it or not, God is heavily intertwined in this entire experience, and so when the pressure of society kicks in to be something other than yourself, you not only forsake your truth and your goodness, but you also set aside everything powerful that is associated with God. I am talking about strength, miracles, compassion, healing, and resilience.

Perhaps we were all too young and naive to even realize that we would have to lose a part of ourselves to meet the demands of life. The greatest cost of being in an organized society has to be the internal conflict that sets in. It is the battle between two energies, one that is spiritual, free-flowing, and unconditional, and that of the world, which is shallow, strenuous, and restrictive.

We stop being ourselves, climbing trees, and listening to God because we are convinced that our worth is tied up in the hustle, performance, and compliance. There's a sharp reality that kicks in once we figure out that we have to meet certain expectations, perform certain duties, or fulfill obligations just to earn love and acceptance. Perhaps it is then that we decide that the world is no longer magical.

I often think about that young person who feels so much light and freedom and then realizes that who they are doesn't work for the rest of the world. This is when "the unraveling" begins. We pick ourselves apart. That small child that once experienced complete love and acceptance must now work within certain social outlines and adhere to different chains of hierarchy.

Now, you may not have the recollection to note when this change happened in your life, but at some point, you had to determine which parts of yourself were safe to reveal and which things had to be hidden, and therein lies the challenge for human beings. We must learn to stay real, retain our innocence, and keep some allegiance to ourselves, emotions, and spirituality.

Sadly, in all of our social conditioning, there is a significant loss of self that takes place inside us, but nobody really talks about that. While we may have once had some reasonable relationship with society, the world has created an extremism in which we have to constantly choose social compliance over authenticity. This book is not only about finding Grace but also about setting realistic goals for yourself where you don't have to abandon your feelings, ideas, patriotism, spirituality, or freedom just to fit in.

Understanding the unraveling of self is integral to your inner peace because you begin to understand how fear can take you away from your spirituality, authenticity, joy, self-love, and free expression. This book is already teaching you to be gentle with yourself and embrace your vulnerability. This is the essence of Grace. And so here we are ... slightly more curious than yesterday and willing to go deeper into this self-inquiry.

- Could it be that those parts of yourself that were shut down a long time ago hold a lot of answers for your inner peace?

- Does acknowledging **"The Unraveling"** give you more insight into certain emotional patterns and habits in your life today?

- Is it possible that the rediscovery of your true self could open the door to your physical and emotional healing?

- Might there be some truth to the fact that you have been trying to juggle and manage so much all on your own?

- Do you see how Grace can assist you in maintaining your energy and give you permission to be your complete self?

So, what do you think would happen if you brought your entire self forward—your curiosity, your messy story, your inner child, your unexpressed gifts, heart, talent, imperfections, aspirations, and faith? Well, the answer is quite simple. You will experience more peace, freedom, and choices in your life. You will feel stronger, happier, and more aligned with that amazing child who arrived on this earth with so much love and light to share.

It's true that we all want to be seen, loved, and heard, but that won't happen unless we are willing to embrace our full selves. We need to go into each room of our house to have full clarity of what we need and cherish. Society holds a place in our lives, but so much of our energy is dedicated to the **SMOKE** and the false ideology that we must earn acceptance.

Consider this moment your invitation to reconnect with that magical part of yourself where you are already loved, your spirit is at ease, your jaw is unclenched, and your heart is untethered. Yes, let us go back to the very beginning, where you were curious and free, for that is where you radiate joy.

Stay Magical.

Love,

Krista

Personal Reflection/Drawing Exercise

This next exercise requires two blank sheets of white paper, a simple box of crayons, your phone to set the timer, a pen, and your journal.[10]

This is a three-part exercise. Because you will be drawing, there may be a part of yourself that wants to treat this like an art project. However, this is a free-flowing exercise that doesn't require any artistic skill. There is no need to identify yourself as a "Good Artist" or "Bad Artist." The greater purpose of this exercise is to allow color and images to fill the page and tap into your free-flowing energy. Refrain from labeling yourself. This is an exercise that you simply cannot do wrong.

Part 1: Put a small #1 in the upper right-hand corner on one of the blank sheets of paper. Now, set your timer for six minutes. Use your crayons to **draw yourself as a young child.** You may interpret this exercise in any way that you want. Hit start on your timer and color until the six minutes are up. You will need to stop drawing or coloring when the timer ends, even if the picture doesn't feel finished. Then, turn your paper over and set it aside for the second part of this exercise.

Part 2: Put a small #2 in the upper right-hand corner of your blank sheet of paper. Now, set your timer for six minutes. Use your crayons to **draw yourself as you see yourself today.** You may interpret this exercise in any way that you want. Hit start on your timer and color until the six minutes are up. You will need

---

10 This drawing exercise has been adapted from the toolbook from the Mind-Body Medicine curriculum. It has been modified for this exercise to connect with your younger self.

to stop drawing or coloring when the timer ends, even if the picture doesn't feel quite finished.

Part 3: Place both drawings in front of you and take in any observations that you may have about yourself as a child or as an adult. Notice colors, emotions, symbols, proportion, etc. Perhaps you noticed a change of energy in drawing yourself as a young person versus drawing yourself as an adult. Feel into your drawings. Once you are done observing your drawings, pull out your journal and answer the following questions:

Is there a particular activity you loved to do as a child?

What advice does this young child have for you?

I invite you to tap into the wisdom of your younger self. Can you see or feel any emotions coming through? Whatever they are, let them be. This is likely to spark a new inner dialogue with you and your younger self. Write as much or as little as you would like. Do this until the exercise feels complete to you. The purpose of this exercise is to give you another level of insight into your younger self and allow you to reconnect with his/her energy. Once you take time to compare the two drawings, you may be able to make some clear distinctions about how you have changed over time.

This is all a part of your self-discovery. There is no need to solve anything ... just love yourself where you are. Part of your healing journey is understanding that you are not separate from your younger self. While you may have had to become more serious and regimented over the years, it's important to connect with that free spirit as often as possible. You are invited to bring forward that playfulness and curiosity that was characteristic of your childhood. Sometimes, our healing is realized once we acknowledge that something wholesome was lost along the way.

Chapter Three

Inter-FEAR-ence

*N*ow, you might be wondering how you can possibly tap into Grace when human beings are experiencing more stress than ever. We are seeing the world go through massive shifts. One cannot ignore war, political division, economic problems, or the rise of mental health problems, and let's not forget how a virus became center stage to a public health crisis.

In this life, we are not only asked to take care of our personal well-being, but we must find constructive ways to process the extreme energies that reside in the world. That's been overwhelming for a lot of people. It is no coincidence that we are seeing a rise in depression, suicide, homelessness, gun violence, addiction, and identity confusion. People are resorting to extreme measures to release themselves of their anxiety and inner turmoil.

So, how does one make sense of these problems that are so broad and immense? Well, that is where our spirituality comes in. When there's stress and massive chaos happening at the same time, it signifies that change is unfolding. This is when we are invited to do some soul-searching. We must observe our present condition and evaluate whether our priorities are in or out of alignment with our hearts and values.

While many of us try to resist this process, it's critical to ask ourselves what the guiding force behind our decisions is. Is it fear, or is it love? All situations that are wrapped in fear present an opportunity to bring in more empathy and compassion. We are all managing intense energies right now. Some people are feeling overwhelmed and on edge while others are feeling optimistic.

It does beg the question, **"What is the underlying difference between feeling hopeful and powerless?"** The answer is faith.

We are questioning so many things right now—the system of government in place, the social structures, and the legal process that have revealed corruption and disparity of treatment. We are currently reevaluating how we take care of one another as human beings. It's not a coincidence that things around us have changed. There is a decline in human health and happiness. It's directly related to people feeding their egos instead of their hearts. We are so consumed with our social identities that we have lost our spiritual identities.

There is an awakening taking place right now, and even if you're not quite sure what those terms mean to you yet, I can assure you that human beings are realizing how polarized we are and how disconnected we are from God. We currently have a spiritual void, and there isn't a single thing that we can earn, purchase, or click on our phone to make it better. It's going to require us to slow life down, go inward, and turn the light on in places that are otherwise considered dark and off-limits.

Our survival behaviors and social patterns are not only jeopardizing our physical and emotional well-being, they are contributing to the deterioration of a civilized society. Now, that may be a lot to resolve in one book, but I hope to facilitate a process in which you decipher your present opportunity to grow and strengthen your faith. It's amazing what happens when you isolate fear and stare at it for a while. You find clarity about what is yours to heal and what is meant to be released or surrendered.

Of course, we are contending with way more distractions than ever before. Technology may have advanced our ability to do things remotely, but it has also complicated things. We are confusing popularity and superficiality with love. It has taken us backward in terms of human interaction and spirituality. While it would otherwise seem impossible to reverse the effects, it is sparking another powerful movement in which everyday people are getting in touch with their faith.

There's an increase in the number of people exploring self-development and spiritual education to counterbalance the density they are feeling from the world. People are starting to notice how deferring our problems and avoiding deeper conversations have contributed to our stress, sickness, and social unrest. You may ask yourself, **"Is there another way to BE?"** The answer is always **"YES."** However, it will require another level of bravery on your part.

In today's world, we celebrate and idealize things that are counterintuitive to love and spirituality. We have become voyeurs to other people's pain. We glorify trauma instead of finding ways to heal it, we separate ourselves with labels instead of searching for commonality, and we cancel out people who may have alternative viewpoints. Could it be that our righteousness and entitlement have made us more inflexible, intolerant, and selfish?

The only way to evolve personally or socially is to see ourselves and our history for what it really is. We cannot pretend that there weren't mistakes, traumas, or oppression in our stories. It is the acknowledgment of pain that allows us to learn and grow forward. We may not ever approve of certain behaviors, but we can acknowledge that human beings are imperfect. This, too, is part of our journey to find Grace.

We might ignore larger problems that require introspection because we have convinced ourselves that we aren't strong enough to manage them, OR if we wait long enough, someone else will have to deal with them. Well, all this denial and postponement have just magnified suffering and reinforced social division.

We keep trying to fix our social problems with power, influence, and money, but those are ineffective because they represent short-term solutions, they tend to be preferential, and they never address the emotional healing that must take place to restore balance and peace. If we want to elevate society and one another, then we must be willing to put in the personal work to become a better person and create a kinder and gentler society.

We forget that spirituality can support us in these tumultuous times. It's the only solution that makes sense at this present time in the world because it is available to everyone. Once we take status, money, and privilege out of the equation, we shall see that we are all the same and have unlimited access to love and spirituality.

It's when we try to navigate through life all on our own that everything becomes overwhelming. However, Grace provides us with a faithful approach to life. It restores strength, fills your empty cup, and engages your higher guidance for support and solutions. It takes into account what is in your highest good, but it also gives some greater consideration to the collective well-being.

We all know it's more challenging to maintain our energy when we're under a lot of stress, but here is what we may be forgetting … **Peace is NOT separate from us.** It's not conditional based on external pieces coming together in a certain way. It is the essence of who we truly are before the world tells us to be something else.

You see, we are the ones that get off track and out of spiritual alignment. When we absorb fear and adopt other people's opinions of us, we are essentially making it a part of our belief system. These assumptions and convictions become our operating agreements, and they guide our decisions. If these agreements undermine our value or self-esteem, they become a detriment to our mental health, spirit, and physical well-being.

The moment that a person accepts the phrase, "You're not enough," they essentially go through the rest of their life trying to prove their value or hustling for validation. This sets up the dynamic where they are always in a state of lack and unworthiness. It's the noise from the world that says, "Hurry up! That's not good enough! You're not safe! Here, hold this fear!"

As soon as you realize that certain agreements you have made with yourself have been sabotaging your well-being and happiness, you can consciously break those contracts and create new ones based on love. Yes, you can bring in something more positive and affirming that supports your joy, health, and vision for a positive world.

It is perfectly within your free will to replace "You're not enough" with "You are loved and valued at all times." Whew! What a breakthrough that would be for so many people who are carrying around somebody else's story of who they think they should be. This book is about reclaiming yourself and releasing any conditionings or traumas that have weighed you down.

The chapters in this book are intended to quiet that inner critic that is otherwise known as fear. You can absolutely remain peaceful and true to yourself despite all the chaos happening around you. You can express yourself without reservation, apology, or shame. You can walk into any situation knowing that you are worthy and that what you feel is important. You can do all those things as long as you commit to an agreement that supports your mind, body, and spirit.

Peace relies on several things, such as being able to express yourself freely, but it's also being able to release yourself from traumatic experiences, expectations, guilt, shame, obligations, bullshit, and other people's judgments and energy. That deep sense of belonging we are all searching for is so powerful and primal. It literally gives us a reason to get out of bed in the morning. However, everything hinges on self-love and acceptance.

If we allow other people to determine our value, we shall go through life searching for proof that we are worthy, and that's an extremely vulnerable position to be in. We are then subjected to everyone's opinions, energies, and approval. We are likely to get lost in comparison and lose sight of the things that make us special.

That habitual need for validation can drive a person mad because one moment, we're up, and the next moment, we're down. It's all dependent on how someone else feels about us. This dynamic is born out of dependency: I need YOU to feel better about myself. It's that shortage of self-love that makes us feel shitty about ourselves, and we are continuously at the mercy of one earth-shattering question, **"Am I good enough for you?"** The most tragic thing is realizing that there is no answer that is comforting to the person who doesn't believe in themselves.

Today's generation is deeply affected by this type of anxiety. We are in an era where both parents typically work, and we give our children an iPad or phone by the age of ten. Now, we didn't realize that by limiting human interaction, we would be reinforcing the influence of social media. It has set up a generation that struggles to make eye contact and communicate their ideas and feelings. It's these collective behaviors that have not only caused an increase in mental health issues, but we are seeing a generation of lost souls who are searching for their identity.

With less human interaction and self-compassion, we are, in essence, averting critical life energy to the earliest primal response known to human beings ... survival. We get trapped in a vicious circle of hiding and protecting ourselves. Human beings were designed to physically adapt and evolve over time, but our expansion has always been so much more than just hunting, gathering, and surviving the elements. We are intended to advance our intelligence, develop relationships, build community, and expand to another level of spiritual consciousness.

When we are entangled in fear, we simply cannot be calm or present. Consider for a moment the energy it takes to hold in your feelings or hide your true self. It activates the sympathetic response and sends your nervous system into survival mode. This makes it impossible to feel comfortable, relaxed, or even excited about life. "Showing up" becomes much more complicated because you are conflicted, "Do I show you who I really am at the risk of being hurt?"

Grace is all about seeing yourself in a kind light where everything has value, including your struggles. You shall see that there are simple tools that you can incorporate into your life right now that can make a tremendous difference in the quality of your health and spirit. At the center of those teachings is learning to breathe into your feelings and your pain.

If you look back in time, you shall see that every great public figure in history has a tale of perseverance in which there is a long, arduous search for something—the meaning of life, fulfillment, peace, abundance, etc. You might say that we are all "Alchemists." We are all on a Hero's Journey to achieve inner peace and self-love. There is no amount of resistance that can alter the Universe's plan for us or the lessons that are intended for our personal growth.

When we shut a part of ourselves down, we allow fear to have some large say in our happiness. This is critical to our human experience because whatever runs **inter-FEAR-ence** with our thoughts, expression, growth, and well-being are just barriers we have subconsciously placed on ourselves.

Consider the possibility that somewhere along the line, you may have absorbed somebody else's pain or shame or taken on a harsh judgment or label of who you are. Now, whether that refers to not being good enough, strong enough, smart enough, thin enough, or pretty enough, that lie keeps you in a closed state. Over time, that story gets bigger and bigger. However, should you choose to see your vulnerability through a compassionate lens, it will activate something very powerful and brave within yourself.

It's true that we live in a highly competitive society where everything is oriented around performance, looks, and materialism. We are often judged and scrutinized by what we do, what we look like, and what we have. However, if it is truly our goal to replace stress and anxiety with peace and Grace, then we will have to release the fear of what others think of us. That's obviously challenging with the presence of social media.

Freedom requires a whole new mindset from us in which we return our power and focus back to ourselves. I like to think of it as an incredible force field where we are consciously drawing courage and inspiration from our inner guidance instead of turning over our well-being to the outside world. After a lot of soul searching, I came up with this definition of GRACE.

> **Grace:** /grās/ *Grace is the universal life force energy that lives within every human spirit. This is your spirituality working through you to bring in unconditional love, positive energy, resilience, and wisdom to every experience. It holds your energy and values in place and seeks a gentle path forward at all times.*
>
> *To be in a state of Grace is to seek the highest good in every situation. It is the honoring of self and the human experience as it is. All situations are gently received, and there is some greater intention to grow through adversity. When aligned with this energy, you can hold compassion for yourself and others. Its alchemizing wisdom can restore inner peace and balance to the outer world.*

People arrive at the decision to heal for different reasons, but a self-reckoning happens. A person decides that living in fear is no longer an option for them. Now, that may represent some dramatic moment. Other times, it's a quiet decision to get ourselves out of bed in the morning. It's that tightness around the throat when someone admits to themselves, **"I can't do this shit anymore."**

At some point in our lives, we must be willing to ask ourselves an extremely difficult question, **"What is running inter-FEAR-ence in my life, and what am I no longer willing to compromise?"** And then we must sit quietly and wait for the answer. As we open our hearts to this new philosophy, we shall recognize just how strong and durable we have always been, and while we may have once thought that our emotional relief comes from the outside world, we realize that faith and self-compassion are the great stabilizers.

Of course, your journey will not look like anybody else's. Keep in mind that everything is rerouting you toward love: love for others, love for God, and love for yourself. There is a wonderful moment in the story of The Lion King when Simba makes a dramatic exodus to escape his fears. After running from himself, he decides to challenge the belief that he isn't good enough or strong enough to lead the animal kingdom.

The Prince of the Pride ultimately chooses to go back to his pack to face his fears. It marks an incredible moment in the film, and you can feel the climactic build-up of courage. The drums start pounding, and tribal music starts playing in the background.

Those drums are so powerful. The pounding creates a reverberating sound that can be felt at the base of your soul. This vibration resembles the sound of a baby's heartbeat. It is somewhat ironic how it symbolizes the journey back to self. It's a fabulous story of triumph where we celebrate the convergence of vulnerability and courage, and while it's just a Disney movie, it highlights the message that there is no amount of fear too great for the person who is ready to take back their power and overcome their emotional obstacles.

In the end, that movie shows us that freedom is often found at the very edge of our own collapse. You might be wondering what it takes to overcome those tumultuous moments. Well, it's quite simple. It takes a decision on your part to love yourself and see yourself as whole, creative, and resourceful. When you recognize that every situation presents a choice between love and fear, you will make stronger decisions to support your well-being, and while there is something primal inside of us that may want to run away, hide, resist, or escape ... we must fight for LOVE.

Well, my friend, it is time. It is time to wake up to our beautiful lives. We are learning to honor ourselves and align our energy with a higher power. This is how you create a sanctuary for yourself. It starts inside, and then takes on a physical presence in your life—in your home, at your job, in your relationships with your partner, children, neighbors, friends, etc.

When we take stock of how stress, fear, or unresolved grief have caused major inter-FEAR-ence in our lives, we can create an environment for peace. Consider this a time of great renewal and acceptance where you are reclaiming what has been misplaced or perhaps misunderstood. In most cases, it is the freedom to be yourself, express yourself, and love yourself. Know that you are positioned perfectly to create a kinder and gentler existence for yourself. The days of devaluing yourself are over!

You can cue the drums now.

This is about to get really fucking good!

Stay Free.

Love,

Krista

Personal Reflection/Optional Exercise

These questions are part of an invitation to go a little deeper if you choose. I recommend that you read the questions a couple of times to yourself and then write something down. Should you feel a little resistance, that's okay. Challenge yourself to stay with your feelings and see what comes forward. Write down whatever observations that you make. You cannot do this exercise wrong.

For this exercise, you will need a pen, two sheets of paper, and a lighter. Dedicate one sheet of paper to question 1. It doesn't matter if you write down just one sentence or use the full sheet. It's not about length. This exercise is about connecting with your truth.

1. What is an old agreement, judgment, or fear that you have been carrying around that no longer serves your health or your vision for life?

When the question feels complete, set it aside. Now, use the second sheet for question 2.

2. Can you replace that agreement with something positive and affirming?

Once you are done with this part of the exercise, study your answers. Notice the energy around each answer. Can you distinguish a different tone or energy? Which one feels dense and restrictive? Now, I want you to imagine how that energy impacts your psyche and your nervous system over time. The object of this exercise is to see how thoughts or beliefs can be repressive. Fear will diminish your confidence and slowly deteriorate your health. It makes you believe that you are all alone.

Now, look at your answer to question #2, your new agreement. It is likely that it taps into a higher frequency. It holds light and possibility. When we consciously raise the vibration of our personal agreements, we affirm more love and flow in our mind and body. This is how we slowly incorporate Grace into our lives. We change one agreement at a time.

The next part of this exercise is optional. Pull out the sheet with your old agreement. Read it and say goodbye. You can crumple it up. You are invited to physically release it in a burning ritual. **(Be sure to do this in a safe setting. You can bring it outside to a designated fire pit area.)** Now, this is a powerful way to release the energy that has created barriers and restrictions in your life. As the paper burns, you will transmute the energy to your positive agreement.

Once the first agreement has been burned and has turned to ash, take a moment to read your new agreement. Read this positive affirmation several times. Invite it into your mind, feel into the words, and lock it in with a prayer or invocation. This ritual is very much in sync with the symbolism of the Phoenix Rising, which represents rebirth, magic, renewal, safety, and transformation. The rising from the ashes signifies perseverance. It is the full circle shift from darkness to light. My friend, this is who you were always intended to be.

Chapter Four

Breathe Easy

I can remember the day I walked into my first class for mind-body medicine training. I was so excited. One of the first teachers to welcome our group was Tanmeet Sethi, MD. She thanked us for being a part of the program and stated that we would serve a significant role in teaching people about resilience. She said, "Once you have a firm understanding of the skills, you will be able to facilitate your own groups and impact your community."

I got goosebumps all over because I knew I was divinely led to this program. Just a few months prior, I woke up with a strange message. I heard, "You will sign up for a training course to assist people in their healing journey." I couldn't tell if it was a dream or a voice, but I accepted that it had to be a higher message from God. I decided to look online to see if anything local fit that particular description. Nothing spoke to me, so I let it go.

I figured that whatever I was supposed to do would reveal itself to me once God thought I was ready. I can remember lighting a candle and saying a quick prayer out loud, "God, I'm pretty sure that you want me to do some formal training to help people deal with grief and trauma, but I'm not sure what that is. If you could direct me on what to do, that would be great." It was short and to the point. Then I blew out the candle and went to work.

Well, what happens when you put your trust in the Universe is amazing. The pieces of the puzzle came together rather quickly. Just a few hours later, a woman who worked for Kaiser Hospital came into our sandwich shop, "Mr. Pickles." She ordered a turkey sandwich and then asked me to use the restroom.

As I walked her to the hallway, she stopped in front of a display with my books and a few copies of *North Bay Woman* magazine. She looked at the cover and asked, "Is that you?" I removed my baseball cap and giggled, "Yup! That's me!" Now, this is where the story gets interesting and, dare I say, magical!

She asked me what kind of work I do in the community. I told her that as a result of starting a community nonprofit, I had the privilege to work with a lot of different people who were dealing with significant hardships and losses. I also shared that our non-profit championed many important social causes like homelessness, domestic violence, mental health for teens, and caregiving.

I didn't realize that I would get so emotional, but I felt a few tears well up in the corners of my eyes. I confessed that their stories of pain, loss, and perseverance affected me on such a profound level. I found myself saying too much. After all, I had just met her, and she just wanted to use the restroom. I quickly wrapped up the conversation and said, "Anyhow, I'm currently shifting my focus toward education and healing."

Her eyes widened, and she blurted out, "Oh my goodness, you need to do our training course!" From there, she described the "Sonoma Community Resilience Collaborative." The program was put together after the 2017 firestorm that burned down several North Bay communities and devastated many people's lives. The intention was to support people in the community who were processing trauma and recovering from devastating losses.

She described the program's vision: "We are currently looking for leaders in the community who would be willing to go through our training program and then facilitate groups to help different people who wouldn't otherwise seek therapy or healing to help them deal with their grief. It sounds like this course could be an incredible fit for you!"

I looked at the woman in amazement and said, "I just prayed for you to come into my life two hours ago." She seemed puzzled, but I knew exactly what was happening. It was no coincidence that she walked into our sandwich shop that day. As far as I was concerned, she was an angel.

In a matter of days, I submitted my application to study mind-body medicine.

I had no idea how this program would change my life, but I recognized two things. God was directing me to this work, and I was thrilled to serve some larger purpose.

My excitement and curiosity led me to do a little research about the program on my own. I learned that the curriculum for the program was based on the teachings of "The Center for Mind-Body Medicine," which had existed since 1991. It was founded by Dr. James S. Gordon, MD, who is a Harvard-educated psychiatrist and a world-renowned expert in using mind-body medicine to heal depression, anxiety, and emotional trauma.

Dr Gordon's extensive work in "Psychological Trauma" has been recognized nationally and globally, and he has been instrumental in consulting White House officials on alternative medicine. He's trained people all over the world to assist with emotional recovery following tragedies, war, mass shootings, natural disasters, and loss of homes, communities, and loved ones. His work would help people deal with the most sensitive hardships known to the human heart: death, divorce, terminal illness, abuse, trauma, and loss of innocence.

As far as I was concerned, there was no limit to how mind-body medicine could assist a person with their healing as long as they were open. After all, everyone I talked to seemed to be stressed out, suffering from grief or anxiety, or carrying some heavy burden. I strongly felt that this type of healing would give people a new pathway to inner peace.

The more I read about mind-body medicine, the more excited I got. It seemed to me that the only real shortage was not having enough people to share the work. I felt humbled that somehow my life intersected with Dr. Gordon because he offered a curriculum to help people transform their pain into something more useful, like wisdom, inspiration, or service. Of course, I wondered how the work would also change my life.

So, there I was, in a room with 75 other people who probably had a cool story of their own about how they arrived at the program. We were about to embark on a brave journey of healing and personal development. Tanmeet opened her arms and said, "The very first tool that we will teach you today is Soft Belly Breathing." I felt a slight panic as I had struggled with asthma for years, and I had just puffed on a rescue inhaler right before class.

While most people don't think of their breath, I thought about mine all the time: my tight chest, constricted airways, and wheezy inhalation and exhalation. However, Tanmeet coached us into a comfortable position. Before she started the guided meditation, she told us that Soft Belly Breathing would become a centerpiece for our healing.

She began the meditation. She invited us to take in a slow, effortless breath. I tried to stay completely focused on her words, but I became very judgmental of myself. After all, there was nothing slow or effortless about me. I was in a rush at all times. I operated on caffeine and chaos. The idea of consciously bringing in calm energy through my breath was the furthest thing from my mind. Honestly, I wasn't sure if I could complete the exercise or the training.

Looking back, I can see that there was something raw and vulnerable driving my life. I had this strange emptiness inside me. I really couldn't tell you what that represented. I had no real name for it. Fear found a home in my psyche. Rather than face or try to understand it, I adjusted the best way I knew how. I just pretended that everything was fine. I figured it was the path of least resistance, but it snowballed into other behaviors.

I sought out all kinds of distractions to avoid my emotions. I even convinced myself that my safety and wholeness were tied to other people. I gave away my time, energy, and sacred parts of myself. As long as I was giving, helping, pleasing, organizing, producing events, or making a difference in someone else's life, I was earning my place in the world. The only trouble was that I was often exhausted, overdrawn, and breathless.

I didn't like myself very much back then. I had no limits or boundaries. I suppose if I had just sat with that empty space long enough, my higher self would have taught me it's okay to feel discomfort because it means that something is getting ready to break the surface and shift. Whatever proof or stimulation I sought had little to do with others. I was just seeking Grace and love for myself.

If I had the courage to sit with that void, I would have understood that everything is temporary and flows through us. It makes no difference whether we perceive it to be good or bad, a reward or a punishment. If pain comes to us, then it has something to teach us. In the end, it doesn't matter whose approval we get if we can't accept ourselves.

From a very young age, I would absorb energy and pain around me. I found myself bogged down with heaviness all the time. I could not separate what belonged to me and what belonged to others, so I volunteered to just carry all of it and call it my own. The biggest problem with being an empath is believing there's no alternative way of being. Without boundaries, we always feel chained to fear, sadness, and unworthiness.

For most of my life, I've chosen to do most things the hard way … by myself. It was that mentality that also shut the door to spirituality. Despite going to Catholic schools and church my whole life, I saw myself as separate from God. This kept me at a very low vibration, unable to see myself as deserving or resilient. I couldn't imagine anything different for myself.

It's interesting how the breath can mirror some deeper void within ourselves. For me, that was the absence of faith and self-compassion. I couldn't seem to breathe in the love that I needed for myself, and I certainly didn't see any higher purpose for grief or pain.

We have all heard the phrase **"Life or death situation."** I now see everything as a **"LIFE and BREATH situation."** As long as we are here and taking in oxygen, we can remove fear and heal any conflict within ourselves. Whatever comfort, relief, or a sense of purpose we believe to be lost can be found in the humble exchange of air coming and going, and every day that we wake up is some confirmation by God that we belong right where we are.

As I stood quietly breathing among my peers, I found new acceptance for myself. Tanmeet continued with the exercise. With her kind voice, she helped me see that I, too, could achieve a calm state with just a few intentional breaths. She invited us to keep our bellies soft and relaxed so that more air could reach the bottom of our lungs to accomplish the gentle exchange of air coming and going.

I absorbed every single word that she spoke and felt invigorated and determined. It was the first time I wanted to meet the resistance that had found a home in my body. Somewhere in that process, my higher self came through and informed me that as long as I avoided my feelings and carried the load of others, I would remain compromised and live in a very shallow existence.

Once the meditation ended, I came to a rather eye-opening conclusion. I never allowed my body to fully inspire, rest, or recharge. I never accepted the support of God or the people around me. I had set up a pattern of rushing around my life, holding my breath, suppressing my emotions, and pretending to be fine. This pattern kept me stressed out, fatigued, and anxious all the time.

This reinforced other codependent behaviors. I became the giver, pleaser, and the overachiever. I put my energy into everything and everyone I could except myself. I felt tears well up in the corner of my eyes, not because I was sad, but because I knew I was in the right place.

This work would help me untangle my messy story and the fears and insecurities I had internalized over time. It finally made sense. I could see why I was physically tired all the time. My poor body adjusted itself around my habits, operating on little fuel, oxygen, and self-love.

There is a saying attributed to Siddhartha Gautama and the Theosophists: "When the student is ready, the teacher will appear." I was pretty sure that God knew that this training program would not only help me find peace in my lungs but perhaps some Grace in my life.

Day 1 of my training taught me the most powerful lessons. **Healing is an extension of my breath. By taking in a full inspiration, I affirm that I belong here and am worthy of love and goodness. I am in charge of my well-being. I get to choose whether I suffer alone in fear or open myself up to spiritual support.**

In the book *The Secret Language of the Body*, shortness of breath represents a feeling of helplessness. A person may feel weak, scared, or disempowered. It may be momentary or a perpetual feeling of complete stuckness where someone cannot express their fears or emotions. This describes a person's anxiety during a stressful or traumatic situation.

This also describes my feelings as a little girl trying to make sense of the dysfunctional dynamics in my life.

There's no separation between our breath, thoughts, emotions, and the survival response. They work off of one another and influence our split-second decisions when we are confronted with a threat or a crisis. If you find a snake on your hike, it makes perfect sense to run, but what if it's the lingering effects from trauma, old wounds from your childhood, or some gut-wrenching loss? Then what?

This is where breathwork becomes extremely helpful. It calms the nervous system, shifts the energy in your body on a cellular level, and brings anything unresolved to the surface. By simply pinpointing what emotions are trapped inside, you can consciously release pain from your body.

It's difficult to take these steps when you're in a crisis or dealing with massive grief, but when you're ready, you can use Soft Belly Breathing to facilitate your healing. Do not underestimate the freedom available to you through breathwork. It allows you to go much deeper to admit to yourself what that trauma is that settled into your psyche.

It may have been too much to process when it happened in real time, but you now have the courage and safety to confront whatever "boogie man" is hiding below the surface. We may not even have a name for our pain until we get in there and explore our true feelings.

The takeaway from this conversation is realizing the relationship between breath and healing. It is in the stillness of Soft Belly Breathing that we are reborn. Minute to minute, we can find safety, clarity, and a deeper understanding of ourselves and the world around us. Our higher power lives in each inhalation, but for those of us who have been clenching our bodies, holding back our tears, and constricting our breath, we couldn't feel the benefit of God's support.

From the moment I learned Soft Belly Breathing, I knew that I would pay it forward one day and teach others to use this tool to support their well-being. It's like an old, reliable friend in today's chaotic world. It connects you to a power greater than yourself so you never feel alone in your suffering. This is extremely comforting, particularly when we acknowledge that so many things are out of our control.

Should you be wondering how to release fear from your life or remove pain or grief from your heart, I invite you to incorporate Soft Belly Breathing into your daily practice. If you have been trying to figure out how to reignite your passion for life, ground your energy, or engage with your spirituality, I invite you to start with one simple gesture—put your hand over your heart and find your breath.

I have a couple of exercises for you at the end of this chapter that will walk you through Soft Belly Breathing. Know that you can do Soft Belly Breathing anywhere and anytime. You can use it as a meditation to start your day, you can use it to intentionally pause during your lunch hour, you can pull over to the side when you encounter something or somebody stressful, or you can close your day with a few gentle breaths and gratitude.

There are no limitations to this exercise, and what is incredible is that you can be in a room full of people and take a few breaths to center yourself, and they would have no idea that you are actively taking care of your needs. And so it is. Breathing shall restore you in the most miraculous ways, and it belongs to nobody but you.

Stay Soft.

Love,

Krista

Soft Belly Breathing Meditation[11]

The ideal setting for this exercise is to be in a quiet space. However, many people can tune out distractions and do Soft Belly Breathing anywhere. It is always a good idea to turn off your phone to remove any distractions. The beauty of this breathing exercise is realizing that you can affect your mind, body, and spirit in a very short amount of time. Soft Belly Breathing allows you to relax your body, center your focus, and recalibrate your energy. It takes you out of the survival response.

Now, depending on your location and available time, I have offered three different scripts to practice Soft Belly Breathing. Feel free to select the one that feels right for your present needs. If you are reading the meditation, go through the script slowly. Allow each word to enter your consciousness to get the full benefit. If you are listening to the meditation via my website or a taped recording of your voice on your phone, find a quiet place where you can safely close your eyes and listen to the meditation without disruption.

Soft Belly Breathing—Long Version

Begin by establishing a comfortable position in your chair. Feel your middle back resting against the chair and place your feet flat on the ground. Place your hands comfortably on your lap, by your side, or across your belly. You might decide to place your hand on your heart. Do whatever is comfortable. You may choose to close your eyes or keep a soft gaze on the floor.

---

11 The script for this breathing exercise has been adapted from the toolbook from the Mind-Body Medicine curriculum. Some of the verbiage has been modified to bring in some of my own healing concepts.

Now breathe gently in through your nose and out through your mouth. This is a relaxing way to breathe. It may be a little unfamiliar, but you will get used to it after a little while. Allow your belly to be soft and relaxed. If the belly is soft and relaxed, more air goes to the bottom of the lungs, where there is better oxygen exchange. Oxygen feeds all the cells in your body and improves the metabolism of the working of the cells.

If the belly is soft and relaxed, it helps to activate the vagus nerve. Vagus means "wandering" in Latin. This nerve wanders up from the belly, through the chest, to the central nervous system, to the brain. It quiets the body, slows heart rate, improves digestion, lowers blood pressure, and helps muscles to relax. This also quiets the mind. It reduces activity in the amygdala, a part of the emotional brain that registers fear and anger. The vagus nerve is the antidote to the stress response. It stimulates activity in the frontal part of the cerebral cortex, which is responsible for judgment, self-awareness, and compassion.

One branch of the vagus nerve connects with centers in our brain that make it easier to connect with other people. When you are breathing slowly and deeply, in through your nose and out through your mouth, with your belly soft and relaxed, you are relaxing your body and bringing yourself into balance. You are essentially quieting the "fight or flight" response and improving the function of the nervous, endocrine, and immune systems.

You are more self-aware, focus better, and feel more compassion for yourself and others. This makes it easier to connect and bond with other people, which helps relieve stress. If your belly is soft and your abdominal muscles are relaxed, then all the other muscles begin to relax as well. Perhaps you can feel that right now ...

To encourage this process, you can say to yourself, **"soft"** as you breathe in and **"belly"** as you breathe out. If thoughts come, let them come and let them go, and gently bring your mind back to **"soft belly."** Take in a few more gentle breaths. Notice how calm you feel at this moment and how present you are with your body. As you call your awareness back to the room, carry forward a sense of wholeness and peace. When you are ready, you can open your eyes.

Soft Belly Breathing—Medium Version

Allow yourself to get comfortable in your chair. Place your feet on the ground, and when you're ready, gently close your eyes or find a soft gaze in front of you. Breathe slowly and deeply, in through the nose and out through the mouth. Imagine your belly becoming soft. To encourage this process, you can say to yourself, **"soft"** as you inhale through the nose and **"belly"** as you exhale through your mouth. If outside thoughts or distractions come, let them go and return your awareness to your breath and soft belly breathing.

No matter how often your mind wanders, gently invite it back to the breath. Imagine the breath coming into your body and leaving your body. Notice what you are feeling at this moment as you have courageously come forward to take care of yourself. **Pause.** Feel free to give yourself a few words of love and praise. **Pause.** When you are ready, take in one more breath, and then you may bring your awareness back to the space around you.

Soft Belly Breathing—Quick Version

There will be many situations where you cannot physically separate yourself from people, work, or chaos. This is when you can do a very quick version of Soft Belly Breathing. This shouldn't take more than a minute or two. Find a position that is comfortable for you. You may sit or stand. Imagine a warm color beneath your feet. This color represents safety, peace, and self-love. If possible, close your eyes or find a soft gaze on the ground. As you take in a slow breath through the nose, imagine the peaceful color entering your body through the bottom of your feet and then moving up your legs, through your belly, arms, and torso, and reaching the tip of your head.

As you breathe out of your mouth, exhale through your pursed lips until there is no more air or sound. If it is comfortable for you, imagine a different color that represents stress leaving your body during the exhalation. Repeat this action two to three more times. Once you feel like you have secured a feeling of relaxation and kindness in your body, slowly bring your awareness back to your present space.

Feel free to utilize any of these scripts for yourself. You might want to incorporate some of your own verbiage to make it more personal for your self-care. Some people find it helpful to tape their voice on their phone to fully immerse themselves into the exercise. Upon completion of your meditation, you may cross your arms around your shoulders to signify love and acceptance of where you are at this time.

Chapter Five

With Grace & Ease

*I*n just a few chapters, we've established the growing need to slow life down. Whether it's to breathe easier, decompress, process painful experiences, realign our energy, or connect with our spiritual guidance, there's something within all of us that needs to pull back on the reins from time to time. This allows us to evaluate what is working and what isn't working in our lives.

Most people have the false impression that they must work twice as hard to achieve peace, joy, and fulfillment. I want to challenge that narrative because it may not be about working harder but trusting the emotional process that you are in to take you further along in your spiritual journey. You see, your life experiences are teaching you valuable lessons about holding on and letting go, the risk and reward of vulnerability, and the truths and falsehoods about the world.

Anything that isn't love is a temporary guest in your body. I'm referring to frustration, worry, shame, confusion, stress, fear, anger, and grief—just to name a few. The truth is, you get to decide how long a visitor stays. It would be very brave of you to put on a pot of tea and sit together to unravel the purpose of its visit. However, if you're someone who doesn't allow your emotions to have a place, you'll need to get the guest room ready.

Pain is intense energy that passes through us. It's delivering a message and simply asking for your immediate attention and reflection. If you have some experience of continual suffering, it's because you have not sat with your guest to understand its purpose. In every situation, regardless of heart-wrenching details, pain has the potential to become love and wisdom.

It's because you go through adversity and feel so many different emotions that you are able to grow on the most profound level. The human experience is extraordinary not just because of love but because we have become these amazing victors. We are constantly overcoming personal battles and reconciling difficult losses. There's not a time in your life when you aren't adjusting, reconfiguring, or navigating through changes. There are seasons to everything, and new chapters are continuously being written.

Pain is part of our stories and transformation. That's why we need to let go of all the judgments on ourselves and others. We need to stop imposing drudgery on ourselves. Your life is a gift and needs to be treated as such. Every time things get chaotic, it means something is about to shift. You have the choice to bring in positive or negative energy. Ideally, you can make space for self-compassion.

Think of it as a **"Grace Period"** where you are unsure how to handle a painful situation, but rather than resorting to fear and resistance, you show yourself love, patience, and encouragement. I once heard a quote from a lovely healer in my life named Julie Sanders. She extended a kind blessing on me as I was going through a difficult period of grief. She said, **"Stay in faith and trust the Universe to provide you with the perfect path forward. With Grace and Ease and harm to none ..."** I instinctively answered her with, **"Amen."**

I later saw that same quote on my niece Tory's mirror. It had so much wisdom. I thought, **How great it would be to share that quote with others.** I loved what Julie taught us. I wrote it down on a Post-it and taped it to my bathroom mirror to remind me that everything is transitional and what I tell myself is very important. We may be making false announcements or imposing additional drama on ourselves by saying, "Life is a grind, a mess, or a complete shit show!" The truth is, if you invite Grace and Ease into the moment, the pain will subside, and the confusion will slowly go away.

It's perfectly normal for us to express frustration, confusion, anger, or sadness when life throws a crisis our way. We may not know what to do with our emotions or what the path forward looks like, but this is when you can let go of trying to figure out your life all by yourself. Turn it over to God, and remember that something is about to shift. Just remember that simple phrase, **"With Grace and Ease and harm to none."** The more you trust, the more likely you are to rise in some beautiful way.

Pain is absolutely a part of life. We all seem so shocked when it visits us. Just know that you're not intended to stay in it for very long. The ebb and flow of life gives us some contrasting experiences and wisdom to understand the human condition. What is the sensation of pain and joy? How do we experience it within our bodies, and what are the emotions associated with these experiences?

As human beings, we don't spend nearly enough time thinking about the benefit of having variance, but it absolutely enriches the human journey, and it takes us further along in our spiritual transformation. If you believe that life is always hard, I want to invite you to see things through a more compassionate lens. If you stop judging and labeling yourself, you will see that you are presenting limits on yourself.

What would it be like to use less force or take away some of the resistance you feel in your mind or body? What would it be like to release density, darkness, grief, stress, anger, obligation, guilt, shame, or any other heavy burden that has taken residence in your thoughts or nervous system? What would it be like to fully let go of the tapes and memories that play over and over in your subconscious, and what would it take to isolate an experience, give it a name, and say, **"Here, God. Will you take this?"**

This is when people are likely to contract, run away, isolate, or self-medicate. They might believe it's easier to hold things in, but not according to their bodies. When pain comes up, they avoid it, distract themselves with work or other people, or they just check out. However, Grace is about tempering everything down to a manageable pace, leaving room for something positive to unfold, and trusting that there is a greater purpose unfolding with each obstacle.

It's one thing to carry our own stress, worries, or grief, but what if I told you that many people are holding onto problems and emotional conflicts that don't even belong to them? This is where empaths (a person highly attuned to the feelings and emotions of those around them) have an extremely challenging time. If you aren't self-aware or conscious of the energy that you are absorbing, you become a sponge for everyone else's stress, fear, and anxiety. You take on other people's battles, fear, and frustration as if they were your own.

Stay with me because there's a message here for all of us (me too). The Universe isn't asking us to work harder. It wants us to bring in more Grace and Ease. It may be asking for us to breathe, let go, or provide space for things to run their natural course. When things become overwhelming, we may default to old beliefs set on lack and insecurity, **"I'm not doing enough."** This is when you are invited to pull over, evaluate the load you're carrying, and ask your divine guidance to support you.

One of the greatest dilemmas is knowing what to hold onto, what to release, and what to surrender to your higher power. I recently held a workshop with my women's group and asked them to take out a blank sheet of paper and draw a line down the middle. I instructed them to use the left side of the paper for *"Part 1."* I invited them to write down as many things as they could think of that they love to do. I called it their **"JOY LIST."**

Once they looked done, I asked the women to take a few minutes to share their list with the person next to them. The women were jovial; they laughed out loud, and the sound in the room got much louder, just talking about the things that brought them pleasure and raised their overall vibration.

It was a simple exercise, but I wanted to remind the women what makes them feel vibrant. **This JOY LIST was part of their great LOVE story!** They talked about happiness, love, peace, contentment, passion, spirituality, and relaxation. They noticed that those are the very same emotions that make them feel alive, real, whole, and peaceful.

Then, I took them through **"Part 2"** of the exercise. I instructed them to use the right side of their paper. **"Now, ask yourself what current problems, stress, or worries are presenting resistance or obstacles in living out your JOY LIST."** The energy in the room dropped significantly. Once I saw that they were done, I asked them to take a couple of breaths and quietly review their list. I informed them that they had a decision to make. Were they willing to compromise themselves and their joy for anything that they just wrote down?

It became clear right away that these ladies were carrying the weight of the world on their shoulders, which was getting in the way of their fulfillment. I invited the women to look through the list again and decide whether their problem was theirs to fix, somebody else's, or if it belonged to their higher power. They used a simple system to identify which category their conflict fell into.

M = Mine: At the end of the day, this is mine to sort through and get my energy in alignment. I need to make the necessary changes and allow myself to be happy.

S = Somebody Else: This is not mine, but I feel sad, upset, or angry that this problem exists. It's time to surrender my expectations and attachments and allow others to do what they need to do to make themselves happy.

HP = Higher Power: This doesn't belong to me, but I have made it my own. My thoughts and emotions are tangled up in something out of my control. It's time to release this and trust the Universe to coordinate changes if necessary.

It was a powerful exercise because everyone, including myself, saw the light come on. When we allow other people and their problems to take center stage in our lives, we change who we are. We become dense carriers of pain and sickness. We become these resentful martyrs because we think we are the only ones who can solve other people's problems.

Believe it or not, this is a learned behavior that is tangled in codependency and survival. The more observant you become of this behavior, the easier it is to change and free yourself from emotional habits that are contradictory to self-love and inner care. If we carry other people's problems and energies all the time, we stay in the stress response, and we never have enough time or energy for our joy. The stress becomes a distraction or some operating excuse for not being happy, healthy, or purposeful.

This exercise was so powerful, and it highlighted the importance of doing a personal inventory. At the end of the day, the way that we impact others is by the example that we set. Being authentic and maintaining self-love is **"The REAL Hero's Journey."** We think we have to slay dragons, solve world peace, take on all of our family's problems, and cure cancer, but at the end of our lives, people admire those who love deeply, show courage, use their **"God-Given Gifts"** and live out their JOY LIST.

Stay Joyful.

Love,

Krista

Exercise & Reflection

For this exercise, you will need a few sheets of blank paper, a pen, and a couple of crayons or markers (yellow, blue, and green).

PART 1: I want to invite you to go through the same exercise I talked about in this chapter. You're going to make a **"Joy List."** Take out a blank sheet of paper and draw a line down the middle of the page. On the left side, list as many things as you can think of that bring you joy. You are not limited to any number. Write down as much as you want. However, I invite you to focus on activities that are just for you. What are the things that give you peace, relaxation, and joy outside your role with others? Just keep writing. If your list is too big for your paper, use another sheet to continue.

PART 2: Once you feel like you've got a good **"Joy List,"** pop over to the right side of your page and write down all the things that take away your energy from doing things on your **"Joy List."** The things that you write down might represent responsibilities, obligations, problems, conflicts, health issues, or concerns and worries for the people you love. Write as many as you can think of. When you feel done, take a few deep breaths and then read your list.

PART 3: Now, you will use that simple code that I talked about earlier to determine who the rightful owner of each thing you wrote down is.

M = Mine: At the end of the day, this is my responsibility. This either serves me in my life or it's here to help me learn and grow. It's up to me to realize its value. If it's a struggle, then I need to sort through my emotions and get my energy in alignment. I may need to make some necessary changes in myself to be happy.

S = Somebody Else: This is not mine, but I feel sad, upset, or angry that this problem exists. It's time to surrender my expectations and attachments and allow others to do what they need to do to make themselves happy.

HP = Higher Power: This doesn't belong to me, but I have made it my own. My thoughts, emotions, and energy are tangled up in something that is out of my control. It's time to let this go and trust the Universe to coordinate changes if they are necessary.

Once you have assigned a letter to all the things on your list, take the ones that are labeled **"M"** and highlight those in yellow. These represent your responsibilities and areas of focus and require your unconditional love and attention.

For the things on your list that are labeled **"S"** take a moment to acknowledge the person it belongs to. It's time to send them your love and positive intentions on their journey. Feel free to place your hands on your heart. As you release this problem, call back your energy to your heart and ask for calm energy for all concerned.

By doing this exercise, you are not taking the position to love them any less. You are simply realizing your boundaries and acknowledging what you do and don't have control over. Now, take your blue marker and draw a line through the things that are somebody else's problem. You will see that your list is starting to become smaller.

Now, take a moment to look at the things on your list that you labeled **"HP."** You shall see that the problems that are immense in your life require spiritual guidance and love. They may not be-long to you, but they are affecting you. The fear associated with them keeps you at a lower frequency, and it's compromising some part of yourself.

As you offer up this list to God or your higher power, take note of any emotions that you are feeling. Now, take your green marker and draw a line through the things that you are surrender-ing. These are still important to you, but you will no longer allow these problems to drain you or interfere with your well-being.

PART 4: Once you have whittled down your list, you shall notice some relief from this exercise. This is the power of discernment in which you recognize what is yours, what belongs to somebody else, and what belongs to God. You are letting go and allowing Grace and Ease to replace fear. Some people refer to this process as **"cord cutting."** You release the energy and attachments to peo-ple, places, objects, traumas, and beliefs that are detrimental to your health and forward progress.

The two most important pieces to cord cutting are letting go and replenishing yourself. You can do this by setting high vibrational intentions. Once you cut the energetic cord from a negative expe-rience or person, you must call back what was lost. It could be love for yourself, joy for your soul, harmony in your body, peace in your thoughts, etc.

Here is a very short prayer that I have created. I have also person-alized this passage to invite Grace and Ease into your life.

"Loving Universe,

Please assist me with this process of cutting all energetic cords to this person, place, trauma, or memory. I restore positive energy to my mind, body, and spirit. I recognize the value of this experience and have opened myself up to restoration, healing, and spiritual growth. I am cutting this cord with a full heart, knowing that all will be well. I call back all that was lost by this experience. I release any ties that bind us negatively. May all cords be cut, trans-muted, and dissolved. May all energy be returned to its right sender. I invite Grace and Ease into my heart so that I may focus on my well-being and joy. Help me heal all wounds from the past or present and restore my physical, emotional, psychological, and spiritual well-being. I ask that this is complete and sealed in love and acceptance.

And so it is."

To BE or Not to BE

*T*here's an irony in trying to keep up with everything and everyone; you lose your true self. When people don't feel worthy or safe they are likely to take on unnatural behaviors and social masks. If we look deeper into human behavior and question why it's become more difficult to be authentic today, we shall see that the answer is **FEAR.**

There are way too many people who have bought into some narrative that they aren't good enough or that it's more important to earn acceptance than to remain true to themselves. As a result, too many people have abandoned their internal compass (heart, spirituality, and intuition) to buy into the noise, division, chaos, and social expectations.

It's the constant need for validation that has derailed many of us from truly knowing ourselves, loving ourselves, and having a deeper relationship with our higher power. When we focus all of our energy on the external world, we become complacent and, dare I say it, intellectually and spiritually lazy. We stop being free thinkers, listening to our intuition, and questioning the things in the world that go against our morals, values, and spirituality. We just fall into social programming that makes us believe that we are powerless.

This mentality keeps us small and defenseless. It diminishes our inner light over time. Sadly, if you ask people where they actually fit in today's world, most people have no clue. So, here's a question, **"What exactly is it that you are following, and has it helped you grow or set you back in terms of your peace and well-being?"**

Most people aren't aware of how fear holds them back. First and foremost, it convinces you that you are stuck and all alone. It leads you to believe that you have no other choices available to you, and it draws you into a false existence where you abandon your faith, values, and instincts to subscribe to a narrative outside your belief system. This leaves you with a very strange void where you feel vulnerable and unsafe.

I referred to this as **"inter-FEAR-ence"** in the last chapter, and it's important to recognize that anything that pulls you away from your core beliefs, spirituality, and safety is a risk to your spirit and well-being. Whether it's the influence of a person, institution, ideology, or social bandwagon, just know that fear is behind all this division and extremism that we are witnessing in the world, and it's nothing like we've ever seen before.

How many of us have recently felt our wholesome values are slipping away? How many of us wake up to our lives and wonder, **"Is this really all there is?"** It's shocking that so many people admit to feeling anxious and lost. Sadly, the common denominator is fear. When fear dominates your thoughts, you experience a loss of self-confidence. It makes you believe that the foundation that once held and protected you is no longer available to you.

The problems that we are facing in today's world have many layers to them. This didn't happen overnight. The world has exchanged consciousness for instant gratification. We have aligned our energy, thoughts, and priorities with people and ideologies that lack substance and integrity, and we've found ourselves lost beneath everyone else's problems. The time we pour into these dilemmas and falsehoods takes us away from knowing our true selves, expressing love, learning new things, exploring our magic, and strengthening our spirituality.

This void represents the departure from self and spirituality. It is the harsh reality that we have given into the fear, and now we live in a world we hardly recognize. Sadly, it's not just our government that is divided. There is separation happening on a community level, in workplaces, neighborhoods, amongst friends, and in families too.

I find it rather perplexing. How is it that we are more divided than ever? Everyone seems to be scraping the world for love, yet it is the most abundant energy available to us. What is this new reality that we've created, and have social conditioning and inter-FEAR-ence changed the entire landscape of the world?

These questions affect us subconsciously because somewhere in our psyche, we know that society can do better. This has created so many conflicts, and as a result, people are confused about where to place their energy. It's quite interesting—those who follow the crowd aren't necessarily happier or more fulfilled, and those who defect from the majority are seen as part of a growing resistance.

It doesn't matter where a person stands on love, war, social problems, justice, sexuality, or politics; there are labels in place for everyone, and it has taken us further and further away from love and our common goals. Sadly, the very thing that unites us is spirituality, and that, too, has been demonized. I suppose everything boils down to one very critical question, **"Who are we, and what have we done with God?"**

Over the last decade, extremism has come into play that we have never seen before. People would rather adhere to power structures associated with technology, social media, marketing, and political propaganda than work on their inner selves. This social machine is fueled by greed, ego, power, and self-serving agendas, and it has completely shaken the fundamental values that support the human collective.

This explains why so many people don't feel it's safe to BE themselves anymore. We are asked to conform to society's rules or risk being shamed, canceled, or excommunicated from groups. The problem is that people are now being shunned for voicing their opinions, beliefs, and individuality.

Society may try to convince you that you don't need faith; you just need a bigger house, a better car, more followers, a slimmer stomach, or a higher-paying position, but that is a complete denouncement of who we really are. There is something spiritual within all of us that is intuitive and wise. It is the essence of who we are, and we do not just dismiss it. Spirituality is our whole reason for being, and it is foundational to love, self-care, healing, connection, and preserving goodwill amongst all human beings.

We have become so intolerant as a society that it's difficult to see what our common goals are anymore. Think about how this dynamic forces people to take sides on everything. It makes it impossible to find common ground and unifying interests. Sadly, we can no longer debate issues. Do you remember when your uncle and father would sit down at the dinner table, have a beer or a cup of coffee, and talk about sports, labor unions, and world policies? They could hash things out for hours, disagree on some things, and still hug at the end of the night.

In today's world, people who don't agree with us become our adversaries. Sadly, this affects our ability to share different perspectives or come to a compromise on issues that affect all of us. Have you noticed a major decline in round tables, negotiations, or peace talks? Everybody is flexing their muscles. Here's what I mean by that. There are way too many people who use force, resistance, or domination to get their way, or they cancel, ostracize, or withdraw their love and support as a way to assert their position or ideology.

The rules of human engagement have definitely changed. Some of this can be attributed to the introduction of the phone and technology. What has advanced society in one way has hurt us in another way. For me, there is a deeper concern. We are losing that counterbalance that grounds us and humanizes every problem. Spirituality gives us a conscience; it allows us to play fair with one another, find a middle ground, and express love and acceptance for all of our fellow human beings.

Unless we are willing to turn the ship around, we are in jeopardy of abandoning the human skills that make us good listeners and problem solvers. We cannot be threatened by individualism. We aren't meant to be exactly the same. Acceptance is part of our spiritual process, and as we evolve, we shall elevate our human experience.

The truth is we can listen to alternative viewpoints without feeling defensive or intimidated, we can be inclusive and empathize with others without taking away anything from ourselves, and we can show compassion, admit mistakes, and apologize for hurting one another. None of those things hurt us. There is no personal cost to any of those things. These are the experiences that help us grow on a personal level while advancing our collective goals and interests.

Life is not a social experiment. Harmony requires us to check our egos and become more heart-centered. As a society, we have gotten used to compartmentalizing our emotions, but this habit desensitizes us. For that very same reason, it's important for you to know how you feel and what you believe. If you were to ask me how we got to this strange place in the world, I would say that there are way too many people who have replaced their divine guidance with social pressure and fear. This is why we have so much chaos right now.

We have lost sight of what matters, and as a result, we have global conflicts, a serious mental health crisis, an increased number of youth experiencing identity confusion, and we can't seem to resolve social problems that are so basic to our safety and human welfare. Sadly, I know this weighs heavily on many people's hearts.

I see it as a spiritual crisis, which translates to a human crisis. As a whole, we aren't dealing with our shit very well. We aren't managing our fear, taking care of our emotions, mending our conflicts, or healing our pain. We're just carrying around all these bags of weight. When you also take into account how busy, distracted, and stressed we all are, we expose another harsh reality: we are becoming a soulless society.

So, how do we bring back respect for human life, how do we become more inclusive, and how do we preserve the safety of all human beings? How do we get back to LOVE?

Everything in my heart tells me that we must be REAL again. We must HEAL that part of ourselves that has resorted to survival and forgotten about the power of love. If we don't raise awareness of these issues, we will see a dramatic decline in the quality of life that we live, and every generation after us will suffer greatly. Case in point ... it would not be reasonable for you to take on all of the world's problems, but by assuming responsibility for your own healing, you shall raise the current vibration that affects all of us.

By choosing to be the greatest version of yourself and committing to your growth, you become a beacon of light for others who are struggling. You see, once you recognize that the media, the political system, and the social machine have no real investment in your growth, happiness, or fulfillment, you can call back your energy and dial into the things in your life that actually matter.

I'm sure God is patiently waiting for us to come to our senses. There is a lot on the line right now: authenticity, civility, safety, spirituality, our liberties, and the freedom to BE who we are, which is why I can make a strong case for healing. We need to know how to release that anxious energy from our psyche and bodies so that we can focus on our priorities again. It's true our problems may not be solved overnight, but every time someone chooses Grace for themselves, something else in the world heals.

I often imagine what it would be like for the world to be calm and peaceful, but to get there, it would require all of us to take responsibility for our own healing. Just remember that as uncomfortable things come to the surface, new possibilities emerge. It has been a habit for many of us to find comfort, relief, or distractions outside ourselves, but the path forward doesn't begin until you look inside yourself.

In the end, it's owning our history, belief system, and spirituality that allows us to be ourselves completely. Should we detract from this bedrock, we will lose sight of our entire purpose for being. Before reading this book, you might not have thought about how your healing is intertwined with your higher power and the energy that you absorb from the world, but it is. We are not separate; we are bound together, but you can decide which frequency you will draw from.

To BE yourself, you must LOVE yourself. I encourage you to make a contract with yourself to focus on your well-being and authenticity. From there, every aspect of your life gets better. So, how do you go about making this commitment? Well, you can do this by looking in the mirror and stating your intentions out loud; you can write in your journal, you can speak to your higher power in prayer, or share it with a loved one. You are essentially trusting your higher self to take you to another level of consciousness and wellness.

With that decision comes another decision to release fear and the need to be in control. It's okay that you have not figured out life completely. Remember, it's a long, arduous journey to become, but once you commit to faith, self-love, and self-discovery, you quickly realize that most of the obstacles that are in front of you are self-created. This is why you cannot get attached to just one way of being.

As you know, life can change rather quickly. Energy is constantly shifting, people are coming and going, and our human experiences are teaching us new things about ourselves. If you can stay flexible and open to change, you will see that the Universe is always conspiring in your favor. You will change. See those changes as an act of self-love and courage, and that's a great thing. Just remember that your higher self wants you to evolve and heal anything in your thoughts or body that is counterproductive to wellness and harmony.

Anything that is left unhealed will subconsciously nag at you or take you through some new trial in your life. In many ways, it's your higher self saying, **"Okay, it's time to lighten the load and release this emotional baggage that has accumulated over time. It's taking up way too much space in your body, in your mind,**

and in your life." Your REAL self holds the wisdom to take you through the healing process.

In the interest of staying true to yourself, I have come up with a number of questions that will help you determine whether you are caught up in fear, past traumas, or social influences that may be draining your energy. (I suggest writing down your answers in your journal.)

- Is there any part of you tangled up in regret, frustration, or sadness right now? If so, what is that experience or trauma that is unresolved?

- Is it difficult to turn off your phone, social media, computer, gaming, or TV? On average, how much screen time would you say you have in a 24-hour period?

- Do you overextend yourself to the point of physical or emotional exhaustion?

- Does grief or fear control your life in such a way that you have trouble making decisions or moving forward?

- Do you find yourself watching too much news or getting sucked into political drama? What emotions describe your experience of the media?

- Do you feel compulsive about doing any one thing? If so, what is it?

- Do you get overwhelmed easily? If so, what are you worried about right now?

- Do you have a difficult time saying **"No"** when you find yourself doing things out of guilt or obligation?

- Does work, family, or other responsibilities cut into time for yourself?

- Do stress or fear affect a lot of your decisions?

- Do you put other people's needs, wants, and desires before your own?

- What is the number one thing draining your energy today?

These types of questions could give you immediate feedback on where you might be expending your energy. Anything that takes you out of the present moment, like stress, painful memories, regret, guilt, anxiety, worry, shame, or terror, will activate the **"Fight or Flight Response"** in your body. This not only creates an imbalance in your nervous system, but it takes away critical life energy that you could be investing in yourself.

Whether fear is real or imagined, imposed or absorbed, it has the same effect on the nervous system, and when you feel anxious, there's an immediate need for self-protection. However, as your self-awareness grows, you'll be much more selective about who you invite into your life and where you place your energy. This is discernment, and it gives you the wisdom to know the difference between fear and love.

Being true to who you are, what you feel, and the experiences you have gone through is essential to your well-being. It takes off the pressure to be anything different than who you already are. It promotes feelings of contentment and peace. In reality, we want authenticity from other people, and so we must be willing to require that same quality of ourselves. In the end, authenticity raises our character, builds trust with others, and allows us to be in excellent standing with ourselves and God.

Stay REAL.

Love,

Krista

Personal Reflection

Look at the questions presented in this chapter. If you haven't had a chance to answer them, grab your journal and do so now. I want to invite you to evaluate where your energy is going. The goal of this exercise is to raise your awareness and observe what is currently draining your energy and keeping you in a state of fear.

Once you are done, take time to go through each answer and ask your higher self to give you advice on which patterns or behaviors would be beneficial to change or release from your life. When you are brave enough to reassess your thoughts and re-evaluate your emotional habits, you shall create more space for self-love and healing. I can't think of anything more brave than to be your true self.

For your additional support, you can begin each day by visualizing a protective bubble around you. You can also assign a power color to it (see the color chart below to support how you want to feel). The purpose of the bubble is to keep you grounded and aligned with your values, priorities, and intentions. This informs the Universe and your higher self to guide and protect your energy when dealing with others or managing chaos in the world. This simple ritual can inspire your entire day and support you with love and protection.

- **Red:** Vitality, Passion, and Self-Confidence
- **Orange:** Happiness, Resourcefulness, and Confidence
- **Yellow:** Joy, Optimism, and Creativity
- **Green:** Balance, Abundant, and Peace
- **Blue:** Stability, Calmness, and Protection
- **White:** Clarity, Safety, and Goodness
- **Purple:** Wisdom, Bravery, and Spirituality

Chapter Seven

The Choice Is Yours

We aren't always conscious of how life presents us with choices between fear and love, and so the question to ask yourself is where does your mind go in times of grief or adversity? If you hold in your emotions, then you are likely to attach your thoughts to fear and survival. This is when people are likely to abandon themselves and their inner guidance.

Human beings aren't designed to stay in survival mode for very long. Otherwise, we shall compromise various systems in our body that regulate breath, blood pressure, hormones, digestion, muscle movement, reproduction, circulation, metabolism, and immunity. Most people know this, but it's a different ball game when emotions get involved. You can't just tell someone to get over their pain. They must want it for themselves and be willing to step into their healing.

The first piece of this process is recognizing that pain, trauma, grief, or fear exists somewhere in your psyche or body. Then, you can acknowledge how certain emotions, behaviors, or symptoms have taken you out of balance. I've compiled a list of feelings and conditions representing a survival mindset. I call it a **"Survival Paradigm."** Take a moment to look over the words. Notice how they make you feel. Are there any phrases or terms that resonate with you? Do you hear yourself in any of these words?

This paradigm will give you greater insight into what emotional avoidance looks, feels, and sounds like. You are welcome to circle any words that hit home for you, or perhaps they describe your tangled experience with another person.

Survival Paradigm

FEAR & SEPARATION TRAUMA "I Can't Do This!" DIS-EASE

ABIDING BY A CERTAIN HIERARCHY Disconnect ANGER

Judgment FIGHT/FLIGHT Anxiety TIGHTNESS VICTIM

Feelings of Lack "I'M NOT GOOD ENOUGH!" NO CHOICES! Codependency

"I Can't Breathe!" SEPARATION Messy HOPELESS

Blame & Excuses HIDING WHO I REALLY AM Conspiracy Theories

Self-Sabotage Power Struggles Emotional Avoidance Depression

GUILTY Rescuer / Waiting to be Rescued SHAME SICK NEEDY

Attachment "I DON'T HAVE ENOUGH!" Density Exhaustion

UNSUPPORTED WINNERS/LOSERS RESENTFUL Holding on for dear life

"I CAN'T SLEEP!" OVERWHELMED ALL THE TIME EGO Numb

Addiction to food, alcohol, drugs, shopping, sex, media ... etc

DRAMA + CHAOS UNFULFILLED Feeling Unworthy GUILTY

HELPLESS ABSORBANT TO NEGATIVITY "Unable to BE Myself" Stuckness

PARANOID RESISTANT OVERWHELMED Mood Swings CRISIS

OBSESSIVE HEAVINESS Scarcity SABOTAGE "I'M NOT DOING ENOUGH"

ABANDONMENT BLAME BLOCKED INSECURITY I'm All Alone

Life is happening TO me!

A person may initially defer their pain just to get through a traumatic experience. However, if their feelings are never addressed, this can become a life-long coping strategy. Unexpressed fear, grief, and sadness will tangle up a person's energy and cause stress and inner turmoil. This doesn't just disappear or get better over time. It gets bigger and takes you further away from your true self.

It is well known that "psychological stress" can be a contributing factor to illness, autoimmune diseases, compulsive behaviors, and stress-related conditions like high blood pressure. Sadly, most people who store their pain don't make the connection between what is happening in their thoughts and what is actually manifesting in their body. They look for a diagnosis that may not be there because repressed pain and trauma don't show up on an MRI or a blood test.

There are universal emotions that we all go through—grief, sadness, disappointment, anger, and frustration—and this paradigm will give you insight into how human beings adapt. Survival is triggered by intense beliefs of being alone, unsafe, and undersupported. We saw this very clearly during the pandemic. There was an unprecedented amount of fear, panic, separation, paranoia, and isolation. Many people lost themselves.

This paradigm may answer a lot of questions about why people sabotage themselves, hurt others, or have trouble pulling themselves out of depression or obsessive thoughts. It may show why people put up walls, dominate, isolate, or become passive-aggressive. The more we know about survival behaviors, the more responsibility we can take for ourselves and support the people we love.

Sadly, we are seeing more and more people act out because they don't know what to do with their sadness or anger. Whether it's violence, emotional or physical abuse, addiction, or depression, every one of these behaviors can be traced back to pain or trauma that has been stuffed away or ignored. This is why healing is such an important discussion. Giving people the tools to deal with pain is the only way to restore health, balance, and inner peace.

The human condition presents us with many heart-wrenching situations, many of which are out of our control. Eventually, we'll experience that blow to the gut. It could be a break-up, a divorce, the loss of a pet, friend, or family member, or abandonment. It might be some stressful move, debt, loss of job, a serious diagnosis, a dysfunctional relationship, or even a global pandemic.

These are real-life situations that can knock the wind out of you, and they require emotional skills and a spiritual philosophy to help you understand the purpose of adversity. It doesn't matter what it is; it may not be your fault, you didn't ask for it, and you didn't deserve it, but once pain pays you a visit, it is yours to deal with. That's a hard reality for people to accept, but healing becomes your responsibility regardless of whether you think it's fair or not.

In today's world, we're not just lacking education about spirituality and healing, but everything is competing for our time and attention. We are so focused on technology, drama, and external distractions that most of us cannot figure out what is missing or out of alignment. If every second of your day is tied up in obligations, distractions, or putting out fires around you, then you cannot possibly know what you feel or what is depleting your energy.

We could literally spend this entire book talking about different survival behaviors. However, I'm only going to highlight four of them. This will allow you to identify vulnerability within yourself and help you understand how human beings adapt to emotional pain.

Fight: This person believes that to overcome a threat, they must assert power and defend themselves at all costs. This often shows up as aggressive or controlling behavior. The person may yell, bully others, or fly off the handle quickly. Their volatile temper may be overcompensating for other moments in their life where they didn't feel safe, or they didn't feel like they had a voice or control.

Flight: This person believes that they must escape or avoid any kind of emotional confrontation. They disappear when things get uncomfortable and rush from one place to the next. It's difficult for them to slow down. They assert their control by micromanaging situations. They are often profiled as workaholics, perfectionists, and overachievers.

Freeze: This person believes they must disassociate themselves from anything uncomfortable ... people, conflict, or disagreements. When it comes to decision-making, they often feel stuck or paralyzed by fear. They don't want to make the wrong decision, so they withdraw themselves. They are seen as passive and feel panicked and overwhelmed in low-risk settings.

Fawn: This person believes that they must appease others at all times. This shows up as people-pleasing and placating others to avoid conflict or pain. They set themselves up in codependent relationships and situations where they feel needed. In general, it's hard for this person to receive kindness, support, or love from others because they don't deem themselves worthy.

If I'm being completely honest, it has been a difficult journey to overcome survival behaviors in my own life. I've been a people pleaser and perfectionist for most of my adulthood. I used to think that pain was so personal and others couldn't possibly understand what I was feeling. Now, I understand that the circumstances may vary from person to person, but we can all identify with heartache. What sets us all apart is how long we choose to hold onto our pain and fear.

There are no shortcuts. Some people work through their emotions privately. Others may find comfort in sharing their process. Regardless of what works for you, you'll need to claim it, name it, and acknowledge the emotion around that experience before you can fully put it to rest. Should you decide to deny your pain, it will show up as a different problem in your life or manifest into a physical symptom.

It's true you may not be able to go back in time, but you can educate yourself, shift your beliefs, and redistribute your energy in such a way that it is working for your highest good. Slowing down to address your inner self is a necessary part of healing. At the end of the day, there are always two choices in the room— fear or love.

Some people may argue that they don't have enough time for healing or have too many responsibilities to take care of. Others might have a difficult time saying "No." They don't want to appear selfish or let anyone down. However, this all plays into a pattern in which they choose to neglect their emotional needs and allow others to dictate their worth and happiness.

Sure, it's easier to focus our energy on other people or things outside of ourselves, but in the long run, we just compound our fears and stress. Pretty soon, we can no longer discern whether our sadness is from today or thirty years ago. We can only postpone our grief or sadness for so long before the Universe creates a situation where it's impossible to avoid ourselves any longer. It might be a life-changing diagnosis, an addiction, divorce, loss of a job, or a mental, physical, or emotional breakdown.

We may not realize it, but when we lose ourselves to pain, stress, or **inter-FEAR-ence,** we subscribe to a mindset that operates on lack and deficiency. We start to believe that we aren't worthy of love, support, kindness, or blessings. The only way to shift those beliefs is to get quiet, go inward, and release anything that feels unresolved in your heart.

Imagine a snake coiled for some time and then shedding its old skin. What the snake won't tell you is that it's making room to grow. In some ironic comparison, humans do the same thing. We will have to release some part of ourselves to expand. When you take space for yourself, you are honoring your emotions and setting aside purposeful time for contemplation. This allows you to assume responsibility for your happiness.

There is a sacred gift available to you through quiet rituals. It could be prayer, meditation, writing in a journal, lighting a candle and sitting quietly, walking in nature, going to a religious service, painting, sitting with a cup of tea, soaking in a bathtub, gardening, etc. It's any activity that allows you to connect with your heart and inner guidance. This is when you experience yourself and God on a whole different level. You can receive wisdom and clarity that you would otherwise miss in a state of busyness.

When you do this regularly, you shall see that you are not a victim of circumstance, you don't need to be at the mercy of other people's approval, and you don't have to accept fear as a primary influence. That incessant need to be perfect or prove your worthiness leaves you feeling exhausted. It's the charade of pretending to be okay that depletes you. Life is begging you to get off the fast-moving train and explore your connection with your higher power.

Whether you recognize it or not, you have been fortified by God's love over and over. Should you not feel that support or presence in your life, it's because you have been conditioned to ignore your emotions, and you have the belief that you're supposed to be strong and handle hard things all on your own. That is a typical belief of the survivalist. You may be staying above the surface because you think it's easier to manage, but in the long run, your emotional holding will run you down.

I'm not fooled by the people who characterize themselves as these lone warriors who have to bear their pain alone because I was one of them. As a little girl, I didn't want to burden others or add additional stress to a big household, so I taught myself to hold in my feelings to make life easier. The only problem with that strategy is that life doesn't get easier. The older we get, the more complex our problems become, and when you compound your confusion, grief, disappointment, and fear over time, life can become overwhelming very quickly.

I had that survival mindset for many years. It wasn't until I embraced my faith and healing that new energy and possibilities became available to me. Since then, I've learned that everything we experience, especially pain, is intended to teach us more about ourselves. Our obstacles are helping us expand in the most profound ways. You see, if we aren't shedding our skin on a regular basis, then we aren't giving ourselves room to grow. All that compartmentalizing adds stress and tension to your body, lowers your frequency, and makes you vulnerable to illness.

Your presence on earth is not about your physical output but your soul's journey. The intervals of sorrow and suffering are as important as the moments of love and joy. The same burdens that leave you breathless and vulnerable are the same gifts that make you strong, humble, empathetic, and purposeful. Suffering exists because we are stuck between two places. We cannot go back to who we once were, yet we cannot go forward because we are unwilling to surrender the protection and control.

If we accept the premise that spirituality and suffering are inter-twined with our human journey, then we can eliminate the idea that we were dealt a bad hand or are victims of circumstance. There's an inner knowing that kicks in that accepts the time and order for which things come and go from our lives, and we understand that our time on earth is brief and everything has some greater purpose.

When we accept that our entire journey is spiritual, we can eliminate all that tension and resistance that lives inside our bodies because we know that adversity is taking us further in our understanding of God, self, and the human condition. This is an alternative perspective to survival. It is called the **"Spiritual Paradigm."**

Spirituality can be described as: A sense, belief, or knowing that there is something greater than yourself. It goes beyond the human sensory experience. When you are in touch with this energy, you can explore your infinite potential as a human being. This inner knowing allows you to expand your curiosity. It offers hope and inspiration. This philosophy recognizes the collective whole of which we are all a part. It brings forward gentle wisdom called Grace that encourages presence, reverence, and self-love.

Spirituality keeps you aligned with your priorities and values. It allows you to find inner balance when things around you seem chaotic or stressful. It challenges you to seek knowledge and truth and explore the greater meaning of pain and adversity. It represents a higher state of consciousness and listening in which you align with your higher power and tap into your innate wisdom to heal yourself emotionally, psychologically, and physically. Spirituality encourages you to exercise empathy and understanding. All-inspired action (simple or elaborate) is designed to help you transform and elevate love for yourself and humanity.

Earlier in this chapter, I gave you a framework for understanding the Survival Paradigm. Now, I would like to highlight some terms and phrases that represent a Spiritual Paradigm. Look at this arrangement of emotions, beliefs, behaviors, and habits. Notice how it compares to the energy associated with the Survival Paradigm. Are there any ideas or phrasing in this list that you feel drawn toward? Feel free to circle anything that you are currently inviting into your life.

Spiritual Paradigm

TRUST "I GOT THIS!" **Purpose** FAITH RESILIENCE

GRATITUDE The Highest Good For All SELF-CARE Wonder

HOMEOSTASIS Forgiveness Higher Consciousness WHOLENESS

LOVE & LIGHT "BE" POSSIBILITY COLLABORATION

HEALING Harmony BALANCE BRAVE IMMUNITY

Compassion WELLNESS HUMANITY Interdependency

Expansive JOY Discernment "TUNED IN" CONSCIOUS

Open to the Lesson Presence Curious Equanimity KINDNESS

"I HAVE CHOICES" PERMISSION TO FEEL Spiritual Introspection

RESOLVE Alignment Divine Timing & Guidance Grounded

GRACE "I AM ENOUGH!" Community ABUNDANCE

WORTHY Wisdom PEACEFUL LISTENING Surrender

Mindfulness EMPOWERMENT Inspiration AWE Humanity

Resourceful QUIET Opportunity Awareness CONNECTION

Self-Love FREEDOM UNCONDITIONAL In the Flow REDEMPTION

"Life is happening FOR me!"

If it's truly your intention to take responsibility for your health and well-being, then you must explore the qualities of spirituality that keep you at a higher frequency. It helps you better understand the heart's capacity for **love, forgiveness, awe, wonder, gratitude, joy, compassion, and equanimity**. These highlighted words are specific emotions that provide a spiritual framework for processing life. They can help you maintain your energy and positive relationships and tend to your emotional and physical needs.

These eight emotions bring stability and wisdom to the human experience. If you have a certain problem, you can evaluate which emotions can relieve you and apply it to your situation. This is how spirituality can become a tool for your health. It has the power to shift your energy and perspective to bring in more Grace, and what is amazing about this whole thing is that it is all self-contained. Everything is within you! You just have to be intentional about tapping into your faith and inner guidance.

Let's look at each one more closely.

(These definitions are loosely based on the Dictionary of Oxford Languages)[12]

Love—an intense feeling of deep affection

Joy—a feeling of great pleasure and happiness

Equanimity—mental calmness, composure, and evenness of temper, especially in difficult situations

Awe—a feeling of reverential respect mixed with astonishment and wonder

Forgiveness—a conscious, deliberate decision to release feelings

---

[12] "Oxford Languages and Google - English," Oxford Languages, accessed March 10, 2024, https://languages.oup.com/google-dictionary-en/.

of resentment or vengeance toward a person or group that has harmed you. It can also be applied to yourself to relieve self-punishment over past mistakes.

Wonder—a feeling of surprise mingled with admiration caused by something beautiful, unexpected, unfamiliar, or inexplicable

Compassion—sympathetic concern for sufferings in your life or the misfortune of others

Gratitude—the quality of being thankful, readiness to show appreciation for and return kindness

Recognizing the difference between these two paradigms is beneficial to your wellness and healing. Your internal compass keeps you firmly grounded in love and resilience. More importantly, it allows you to stay REAL in today's world. In every situation, no matter how difficult or grim, you can choose which paradigm you will draw energy from. Will you operate from a place of fear and survival, or will you embrace love and tap into your spiritual guidance?

There's something very freeing about keeping a spiritual mindset. You stop questioning whether it is safe to be yourself anymore, and it doesn't matter what the world throws at you because there is nothing stronger than a person who is firmly grounded in their truth and their faith.

Stay Spiritual.

Love,

Krista

Personal Reflection/Optional Exercise

Now that you can differentiate between these different paradigms, you can identify when you are caught up in fear and survival or when you are connected to your spirituality. It is obvious that the Spiritual Paradigm is better for your physical, emotional, and psychological well-being. It provides comfort, answers, and stability.

I want to invite you to go back and look over the words that you circled from the "Spiritual Paradigm." Every emotion, phrase, or behavior presents you with a positive choice to live with more optimism, grace, and peace. These will help you maintain your energy and support you in times of loss and confusion.

Select several words or phrases that speak to your heart and fill out five "I AMs." I encourage you to do at least five, but if you want to do more, you can absolutely keep going. If you haven't done "I AMs" before, they are simple affirmations that help you direct your focus and energy toward your intentions. They assert your truth and help you create the ideal attitude, environment, and relationships to support your highest good. Keep in mind that the more specific you are, the better.

For example:

I AM Worthy ... **I AM worthy of love and kind friendships.**

I AM Open ... **I AM open to receiving financial abundance.**

I AM Creative ... **I AM creating a home that makes me feel comfortable and safe.**

I AM Forgiving ... **I AM willing to forgive myself for making unhealthy decisions.**

Your turn:

I AM _____

I AM _____

I AM _____

I AM _____

I AM _____

When you get into the habit of using these I AM statements, you will not only raise your confidence and vibration, but you will align with your own divinity. These energy-boosting statements can reprogram negative messages that are encoded in your psyche. They can improve your overall well-being and reach you on a cellular level. These statements are like magic. Whatever positive word you place in your affirmation will enlist the love and support of the Universe.

Chapter Eight

What's in the Box?

*I*n light of these contrasting paradigms, it's good to ask yourself which paradigm you are more inclined to lean on for managing your emotions, stress, grief, and fears. Is it the **Survival Paradigm** or the **Spiritual Paradigm**? This information may be new to you, so it's opening your mind to new concepts that will support your well-being and help you become more self-aware.

From the moment that you learned how to bond as an infant, you have been subconsciously assembling a **"Toolbox."** You have been putting all kinds of things in this magical box: family rules, social beliefs, cultural traditions, parental lessons, and coping strategies. These teachings have nourished and supported you over time, and they have provided a foundation to interact with people and experience joy.

This toolbox has helped you navigate through some rather difficult obstacles and hardships. This framework has provided the values and structure to maintain your interpersonal relationships, solve problems, manage stress, and advocate for yourself. Whether you're aware of it or not, you have been drawing information from that box from the moment you started socializing at preschool.

It helped you make friends, and it supported you when you

bombed your first test and went through your first break-up. It helped you get through school and land your first job. It has basically set you up for life as you currently know it. I find it rather interesting that most of us don't even look in that silly old box. Do you ever wonder what exactly is in there?

Habits and beliefs play such a big role in your self-esteem. How you feel about yourself will determine your health and happiness. This toolbox determines how you filter information—your childhood experiences, mistakes and failures, and any significant loss or trauma that you have gone through. This toolbox is vital to your resilience and spiritual growth, and it's very influential in how you participate in your life and relationships.

As you continue on your search for Grace, you must recognize how this toolbox supports your physical, emotional, psychological, and spiritual well-being. The more personal reflection that you do around this toolbox, the more you shall understand yourself, your upbringing, humanity, suffering, and the role that faith plays in your life.

Spirituality is an unconditional lens through which you recognize your goodness and the value of every human being. It gives you the courage to release any attachments to your old skin. It allows you to cut all of the emotional cords that are tied to trauma, dysfunction, and toxic people. For all these reasons, I invite you to look through that old toolbox of yours so that you can consciously decide what you will keep and what you will release.

After studying these two different paradigms, you're empowered to decide which energy you would like to associate with. This is a critical juncture in your life because you're between the person you once were and the person you want to become. In fact, it is likely that you're in a place where you're pondering some of the most important decisions of your life:

- How do I take better care of myself?

- How do I release anger, resentment, and grief?

- How do I connect with my spirituality?

- How do I manage my fears in today's world?

- How do I bring more love to my relationships?

- How do I work with my emotions instead of resisting them?

- How do I find the courage to address my current health issues?

- How do I find love, compassion, and acceptance for myself?

- How do I make peace with that part of my story that was buried a long time ago?

It's an emotional process to go through these questions, but the investment is worth it because you rebuild trust and establish a deeper connection with your higher self. This process reminds me just how important it is to have a clear path forward. Sometimes, we need to remove all the debris from the road after a major storm. Sure, we could try to pass through, but if certain things are blocking the path, it becomes dangerous and frustrating. Life is a little like that. We've got to clear some of the fallen trees off the road so we can pass through safely and easily.

It's quite possible that you told yourself a long time ago that some things are just off-limits. Maybe you didn't have the courage, wisdom, safety, or support to help you sort through painful experiences, but this marks a new beginning where you are free to choose another course of action. It's all about reframing your experience and bringing in self-compassion.

I call it **"The Place of No Return."** You have the free will and permission to change anything you want ... your mind, direction, beliefs, health, weight, education, relationships, career, lifestyle, plans, and dreams. Nothing is off-limits, and everything is possible. You just have to find the courage to ask yourself that one brave question, **"What's in my toolbox?"**

Stay Curious.

Love,

Krista

Personal Reflection

For this exercise, you will need a pen and a journal to answer a few questions about your toolbox. Release any judgment of yourself or parental influences. The information you draw from this exercise is meant to help you determine what is in your best interest TODAY.

You may have adopted certain behaviors early in your life from authority figures, cultural influences, and social conditioning. Keep in mind that everyone did the best that they could. This is the moment that you can reorganize your toolbox. You can take some things out of your toolbox, and you are welcome to put new things in there too.

1) I want to invite you to go back and look at the Survival Paradigm. Spend a few minutes with it. What are some of the habits, beliefs, or behaviors that you have held onto that no longer serve your best interest?

2) Spend a moment looking over your answers to question #1. It is very likely that you have identified feelings, emotions, and behaviors that you would like to change. Now, review the Spiritual Paradigm. What are some different beliefs, habits, and choices that you would like to install in your toolbox to manage your well-being moving forward?

Chapter Nine

The Big Bang

*O*nce you take the time to identify your emotional habits, you'll have a better idea of whether you're stuck in your head too much, overthinking your life, questioning your worth, and hiding parts of yourself and your story. That habit requires a lot of physical, emotional, and mental energy. It's this survival mentality that often makes a person feel all alone and empty. However, the more time you spend listening to your heart and engaging with God, the more inspiration you'll experience. I want that for you, me, and those people who have given up on themselves.

Healing doesn't happen overnight. It's a process of peeling back the layers of hurt and protection to be real, open, and fully present. This is that moment when I ask you to think about your life in terms of significance. How do you want to be remembered? What impact would you like to have on your loved ones and your community? Have you ever given much thought to what your legacy will be?

The only true regret we shall have in this lifetime is not fully understanding our capacity to give and receive love. You see, people don't sit on their deathbed wishing they had a nicer car or a bigger house … only that they had more time … more time to express their truth, gifts, passion, heartache, forgiveness, and love. Our long-term happiness relies on a greater understanding of ourselves and how our free will intersects with God's will. Now, I didn't make that up. I learned that from my mother-in-law, Catherine, while she was in my home on hospice.

If it's okay with you, this is the point of our journey together when I introduce you to a person who had a massive influence on my understanding of life, death, Grace, and free will. I had her in my life for well over thirty years, but it wasn't until she was getting ready to pass away that we connected in the most profound manner. I would love to share some of her final life lessons. They magically coincide with the message of this book, which is to heal yourself and allow your spirituality to guide you through your journey.

As she was preparing to release her life, she had an interesting request, "Honey, I want you to get a piece of cardboard and pin it to the wall." She instructed me to take a Sharpie and write in bold lettering the words **"FREE WILL."** I did what she asked even though I had a ton of questions. She often directed me to pull out a journal to record her wisdom. It didn't take long for her to convince me they were coming from God. She would say, **"The messages are coming in pretty strong right now. Be sure you have a good pen."** Now, I didn't realize then that she had one foot in my living room, and the other was already in Heaven.

What I now know for sure is that Cathy had a very unique spiritual assignment in those final weeks of her life. In the midst of embracing her mortality, she was supposed to teach us how to live more gracefully. Imagine that—a woman on her deathbed reciting lyrics from God. It happened. It really did happen!

I can remember one particular morning. I had barely made my way down the stairs in my slippers and robe when I heard Grandma Cathy say, **"Get some coffee, Honey. I want to talk with you about something very important."** We had converted our living room into her bedroom. We put up temporary screens to create privacy and hung her fur coats to give the room a bit of her style and character. We decided there was no reason to save anything for a special occasion, for this was one of the most important moments of our lifetime.

We called her space **"The Grateful Room."** Cathy ensured that she told people it was a sacred place and that everyone who enters and leaves her room must be smiling. She became a preacher in those final weeks. It didn't matter that she could no longer get out of bed. She held sermons all day long. She would say, **"In this room, we tell the truth. We only talk about the things that really matter. I want to know your joy and your plans. Please don't leave a single detail out."**

During a period of five weeks, she met with as many family members and friends as she could. She even acknowledged my girlfriends who brought over meal train dinners. She would use the anointing oil the priest gave her from our local church to bless people. It's true; everyone who left her room felt honored by their exchange. They would describe her with such graceful terms: wise, joyful, and spiritual. She operated like a Shaman, and her intention was to enlighten others on their healing journey.

On that particular morning, I sat down with my coffee completely ready and focused on taking notes. I was committed to writing down every last word she had to deliver. I was certain that she had been chosen to be a spiritual messenger, and I was invited to document her process. I kept thinking, *What an amazing privilege to witness this final phase of life in this manner!*

She began, "Honey, you're going to be my Ghost Writer. You're going to take all of your life studies in Psychology, Spirituality, Mind, Body, Medicine, and Energy and blend them with the messages pouring through me right now. Some of it won't make sense until later, but I believe you will unravel the greatest love story ever told."

As you can imagine, I felt a certain pressure. I didn't want to screw any part of it up. I literally asked God to help me listen and retain everything she had to say so that I could properly share it with the world later. I made her a promise that day that I would make sure that her wisdom would find a sacred path to reach people.

I knew that everything pouring out of her was coming from a higher place. She was in an elevated state that I had never seen before. I thought, *How incredible that this 86-year-old woman who appeared so frail and unassuming in her green satin night-gown was so elegant, brave, and precise. She was like a Native American Medicine Woman.*

She then tackled one of the biggest mysteries known to man ... how the Universe came to be. "Honey, astronomers, philosophers, and scientists have always wanted to understand the Universe. They would theorize the moment in time when there was an evolutionary shift. They've always wanted to assign some scientific moment to depict the birth of the Universe. People talk about The Big Bang Theory as if it could explain the cosmic shift in the planets and address our magical existence as human beings. However, they fail to understand the role of God and how everything is here because he decided that we were meant to be."

She continued as if it were some dissertation she had been studying for years. "You see, everything ... the Universe, the light, the stars, the moon, animals, nature, and human life began as a result of God's Love. He wants us to know that his love is boundless and immeasurable. We have infinite light and potential because of that love, and it can only be understood by faith. If someone is struggling in their life or has doubt about their divine purpose, it is because their faith is fractured in some way and their soul is calling for more self-love and spirituality."

I stopped to give her a sip of water through a straw, and she waved my arms away and continued. "Each one of us has been granted free will. You see, between the date we were born and the date we go to our eternal rest, we are gifted with choice. That is what makes life absolutely adventurous, captivating, and utterly glorious. Oh, Honey, everything is possible ... not because of luck, but because we are brave enough to align ourselves with our higher power." She paused for a moment and nervously asked, "Are you getting this down?"

I nodded and took in a couple of deep breaths. I took a massive amount of notes during that time and knew with a hundred percent certainty that she was in a higher state of consciousness. It was nothing like I had ever seen before. She couldn't stop talking. At first, I was confused by her message and behavior, but then I settled into some deeper trust that everything was unfolding with some divine purpose that I had yet to fully understand. I didn't question her. I didn't question God; I just kept taking notes.

Although she had little strength, she was incredibly animated. She used her hands to demonstrate the greatness of the Universe, and then she would rub her tiny fingers together to specify the delicate nature of human life. I made sure not to interrupt her again until she was done. This was not the ramblings of a sickly woman getting ready to pass away. This was some sort of miracle passing through her life and mine. I kept thinking about the awe and beauty of the moment, where I had never felt closer to her or God before.

She continued to teach me about this term **"Free Will."** She brought up all the social unrest across the United States with the riots and protests, she talked about fractured families that have lost touch with one another, and she highlighted the distortion of politics. She informed me that all of those things were just distractions. "Whoever is in office shall have no bearing on how we conduct ourselves, treat one another, or honor our beliefs and values. There are no excuses, Honey. There are only choices."

Then she acknowledged the turmoil of being away from the love of her life, her husband Dan. It broke her heart that he was in a senior living facility dealing with Alzheimer's. Cathy knew that he was confused by the "Covid World," and he was traumatized daily to be without her. She talked about the burden she felt because she could not resolve the world's conflicts or help her husband overcome his confusion. At that moment, she cried like I had never seen before. She grabbed my hand and repeated her love for Dan, God, her family, and her country.

We both wept.

As she wiped the tears away from her cheek, she said that she thought she had to figure out everything on her own. She said that all of that unresolved pain felt so heavy, and the challenging dynamics of her life represented **"The Perfect Storm."** She said, "Noah had a storm; I had a storm. Honey, everyone has a storm, but my greatest liability was holding onto the belief that I had to fix it all by myself."

She then raised the back of the bed forward with the remote control. I could tell that she didn't want me to miss what she was about to confess. "Do you remember the night you brought me to the emergency room? I was in excruciating pain. Krista, I was trying to carry everything all by myself. I had the weight of the world, the sadness of not seeing my family and friends, the fear of Covid, the grief of managing a husband with Alzheimer's, and I had this stupid pain above my heart that would not let up. I prayed that something would give or that God would intervene."

I held onto every word of her story, knowing full well that her painful memories were taking me on an incredible journey. I was so grateful to listen to her story. Without her narration, I could have easily missed important details that made her experience so profound. She continued with her story. "That night in the hospital proved to be a miracle. When the doctors decided to hospitalize me for more tests and help me manage my pain, I lay in that room all alone. I moaned out loud. I was in total fear, and I felt a helplessness like never before. I just wanted to die.

It was not long afterward that the doctor confirmed that the little spot that they identified on my X-ray was a tumor on my lung. There was cancer around my heart."

She confessed that she had a premonition that she would die one day of lung cancer, just like her mother. I was so impressed by her ability to recount every little detail. "Honey, it was not long after I got assigned to a private room that a woman visited me. She had a clipboard and a kind smile. She wanted to talk to me about my nutritional needs during my stay at the hospital. I figured that we would talk about whether I wanted the fruit Jello or the pudding. I had no idea what would come next!"

Cathy paused and put her hand on her heart. "Sweetie, this will blow you away. If you can believe it, her name was Marie, and she wore a beautiful cross around her neck. I immediately told her that one of my favorite angels in Heaven was my cousin Marie. I shared with her that Marie had died way too young because she had breast cancer. We shared a childhood, a sisterhood, a motherhood ... we shared everything. She was the epitome of goodness."

Cathy continued with her story, "I told her that it was so ironic that she was here because I have always felt my cousin's energy throughout my entire life. Krista, she told me that she grew up going to Catholic schools and attended church. It was incredible that we had so much in common. Before I knew it, we started talking about the meaning of life."

Cathy pointed to my notepad, "You're getting this down ... right,

Honey?" I told her not to worry. She continued. "Marie's presence was a miracle, Krista ... an absolute miracle! She may have been assigned to me for patient care, but what she actually gave me was the gift of peace. I think her wings must have been disguised by her blue hospital smock, but believe me when I say it ... she was an angel! She really was!" I told her that I believed her.

When Cathy told Marie about all the pain around her heart, Marie told her that the only way to free herself was to offer it up to God. Marie told her to write down two little words that would change everything for the better. Cathy grabbed a little Kleenex box and scribbled down the two words Marie recited, **"Redemptive Suffering."** She told Cathy, **"Until you surrender your pain over to God, it will remain a burden on your heart, and you will continue to suffer. The pain will cease once you turn over your fear and resistance to God."** She then put her hand over Cathy's hand and bid her farewell.

Cathy said that she engaged in a long prayer after Marie left. She thanked God for all his sacrifices, and offered her pain up to him. A few minutes later, Cathy noted that her physical pain and anguish were completely gone. She then held the empty Kleenex box to me and said, "Never throw this out. It was a part of a miracle. I learned that Redemptive Suffering is how we shall heal our pain and relieve ourselves of worry and fear. Honey, it's everything. It's God's gift for us. It is the way to give ourselves peace when life feels absolutely unbearable."

Despite Cathy's repeated requests to her doctor to talk with her angel, Cathy never saw Marie again.

I told Grandma it was a beautiful story and not to worry because I got it all down on paper the way she wanted. I lowered her hospital bed and suggested that she rest. Before I had a chance to tell her to have a good nap, her eyes closed. I walked out to the porch and felt tears pour down my face. I sighed. I felt so much gratitude for this woman who was slowly fading away from my life.

I knew she had to tell that story and relay God's message. I felt honored to listen. It was not only a higher calling for her but for me as well. While Cathy had no real proof that God's message would reach the larger world, she chose to place her faith in me, and I can't imagine leaving this earth without documenting this miracle for her.

I have a new perspective since I shared that moment with Cathy. For me, she was always this class-act mother-in-law who held her Italian roots close to her heart. Her greatest pride was her family, heritage, and country, and while I once thought her legacy was her children, I have changed my mind. You see, in my opinion, she experienced a miracle during that helpless moment in the hospital, and as a result of her exchange with Marie and God, she was gifted with some greater purpose to change thousands of people's lives.

That holy message may have arrived to a sick woman, but it restored her in the most profound way. You see, we are not meant to bear our pain alone, and yet so many of us become depressed and physically compromised as a result of trying to change, solve, or bear the burden of our grief all by ourselves. "Redemptive Suffering" shall liberate us from all strife and trauma. Turning our burdens over to God isn't some half-court shot or long Hail Mary at a football game. It's not some desperate act but an act of true love, adoration, and salvation.

What Cathy perceived to be a lonely path of suffering was just a self-limiting belief that she had to fix her problems all by herself. I think we have all felt that way at some time or another. By allowing God to be a part of her experience, Cathy was giving herself permission to see everything with more Grace and possibility. This allowed her to bring in self-compassion. Suddenly, my concept of the Universe became so clear, and the idea of watching

Cathy die in my living room wasn't so scary, and my burdens didn't seem so great either.

Once Cathy got out God's message, she felt utter contentment with all she had accomplished on earth. Her physical life was ending, and in the days following, she would stop eating, drinking, and talking. She took tiny breaths until God told her not to.

When I think about how common it is for humans to feel the pressure to fix and solve everything in their lives, I feel so comforted by Cathy's wisdom. What is known as "Redemptive Suffering" is really just some sweet surrender on our part to get out of our head and into our heart. It is a conscious decision to let God share in our emotional trials. By offering our fears, pain, confusion, disappointment, or grief up to him, we acknowledge his unwavering love and his desire to support us in our journey.

Consider for a moment the gift before you. The same creator of the entire Universe that arranged for you to be born has the infinite capacity to hold you during the most painful moments of your life. God not only has the capacity to hold you, but he is holding me too. It is our faith that delivers during times of trouble, and Cathy's story reminds us to remain trusting and hopeful.

My friend, whatever appears sad, confusing, or otherwise inconvenient in your life will shift once you turn it over to your higher spirit. Now, those aren't my words; they aren't even Cathy's words; they are just love notes from God. I find the whole thing rather extraordinary.

Stay Faithful.

Love,

Krista

Personal Reflection

For this exercise, you will need a journal and pen. Take a moment to think about Catherine's story and ask yourself where you can shift your perception of a current problem in your life by applying the concepts of Free Will, faith, and redemptive suffering.

1) **What burden have you been trying to solve on your own?**

2) **What inspiration do you take away from Cathy's story?**

Chapter Ten

The Invitation

When you see the word "invitation," you might naturally start to think about birthday celebrations, dinner parties, social gatherings, or meaningful occasions like a wedding, baby shower, baptism, or even a memorial. Now, I don't know anyone who doesn't love receiving invitations. It conjures up all those warm fuzzy feelings because someone who cares for you has decided to include you in their time of celebration or need. It affirms that we are indeed special.

This chapter marks a very important moment when we talk about your relationship with your higher power. Everybody has some interpretation of what **"The Divine"** means to them. It's okay that there's variation in religious beliefs. In this chapter, feel free to plug in any title or name that resonates with your heart. I affectionately choose **"God."**

So far, this book has challenged you to dive into a greater understanding of your emotional patterns and survival behaviors. So much of what we do is habitual. It's time to take this self-inquiry one step further and determine whether your beliefs and habits support your personal growth. This leads us to a very interesting question, **"How does spirituality currently fit into your life?"**

The Universe creates specific moments for us to go deeper in our understanding of ourselves, faith, and humanity. These experiences are designed to teach us about empathy and compassion. In some cases, we are asked to surrender what is out of our control. These are what I like to call **"Invitations."** When you lean into these moments and open these invitations, you are entrusting yourself to God. You are open to receiving a new spiritual lesson and willing to expand your heart and knowledge.

In sharing these moments with God, you are releasing the need to solve everything on your own.

It's this sacred partnership that makes life such an amazing collaboration. It's how you develop intuition and refine your wisdom. It may be difficult to see it when you're knee-deep in crisis or sadness, but hardships pave the way for new possibilities and growth. This is when you can **"Level Up,"** going higher in your frequency and deeper in your knowing.

The question isn't whether you will go through various obstacles or challenges ... it's whether you are embracing these invitations. There are certain life lessons and emotional traumas that cannot be ignored. The easiest example of this is grief. If you don't open it, you will find yourself stuck in it ... unable to move backward or forward, and you will experience physical stress and emotional conflict.

Sure, there are some situations that you can walk away from with little consequence, but if the pain requires you to process heavier emotions, then you cannot pretend that they don't exist. What may start as a simple invitation could morph into a larger problem, like addiction, or take on a physical symptom or ailment in your body. It's incredible how pain manifests in a person's life, and it's different for everyone.

When you trust the process and open these invitations, you allow space for God to show you Grace and teach you self-compassion. Regardless of the circumstances, if trauma or grief settles into your psyche, then it's yours to open. No amount of avoidance can change that reality. At the end of the day, it's your lesson and your invitation with your name on it.

You will go through a transformation during this lifetime, elevating your frequency and sentience. This is when you establish awareness of what is happening on a human level and what is happening with your internal process. This is what is known as **"consciousness,"** and it allows you to have a deeper experience with yourself, God, the earth, animals, nature, your fellow human beings, angels, guides, and even your loved ones who have passed away.

Some people describe consciousness as **"being awake."** You are certainly aligned with spirituality. Therefore, you can be present, observant, and intentional. Consciousness allows you to view the world with objectivity and place goals in your life that are favorable to all. This mindset supports you in times of stress and disorder and restores balance to your nervous system. It will always bring you back to the center where you can access your inner guidance and make choices based on wholeness, oneness, and safety.

Without consciousness, you are more likely to struggle with stress and changes in your life. As for society, the absence of consciousness makes us lose sight of our greater priorities. This is precisely why we are experiencing more chaos today. There aren't enough people paying attention to their spiritual growth and emotional well-being, so they can't possibly step outside their pain or survival behaviors to plug into the universal vision for safety, peace, or wellness for all.

They say that if something is not growing, it is dying. That is true for the wildflower, the tree, and also the human spirit. Every part of your story is supposed to help you graduate to that next level of consciousness, and it is because you walk through these high and low frequencies that you can discern what is meaningful.

It is estimated that there are about 4,000 religions across the world. We know it's an individual preference as to how people worship and engage with their religion, but I want to highlight one incredible truth. What is understood by your heart is universally understood by all. We think we are so different or superior, but God created us in such a way that our emotions are universal. We are bound together by our shared experiences of love and pain.

Spirituality may not always be comfortable for people to openly talk about. It's because it is so personal, and we need to feel safe sharing this part of ourselves. Most of our lessons around spirituality were passed down to us through well-respected authorities like our family members, teachers, youth leaders, rabbis, ministers, pastors, and priests. I invite you to get in touch with all that is dear to you but also leave the door cracked open for something magical to enter.

Your faith journey is about bringing all that is private and reverent together. Earlier, we talked about assembling a toolbox. It's important to have faith as a personal resource because it's the most effective tool for processing fear, traumas, and losses. It takes you through the healing process, gives you a deeper understanding of life, and affirms your resilience. Without it, you may question whether you are strong enough to handle obstacles that come your way.

So, what are textbooks for spirituality? Well, your life becomes your personal textbook. It takes you through the necessary lessons to understand the power of love, empathy, service, and forgiveness. None of these concepts are ever mastered, so life provides you with new experiences, lessons, and practice. As long as we are all here on this human journey, we not only have more work to do on ourselves, but it's our responsibility to participate in the improvement of society.

When you adopt a spiritual mindset, you not only take ownership of yourself but you also see yourself as part of a solution to heal, inspire, and serve others on their journey. As the world attaches itself to superficial rewards, media platforms, and political agendas, we are tempted to abandon spirituality and one another.

Some of the most challenging problems that we are seeing in today's world are invitations from God to take stock of our spiritual priorities. As long as there is war, homelessness, a mental health crisis, racism, violence, identity confusion, addiction, political separation, depression, obesity, protests, separation, and division, we are invited to pause, think about who we are, and evaluate whether our choices are aligned with our values, beliefs, and hearts.

In today's world, there seems to be a lot of confusion around religion. Spirituality gets mislabeled all the time. Of course, there are positive and negative interpretations. I have often asked myself, **"Why does the belief in a higher power present so much controversy?"** The answer to that question is not in the least bit surprising. There are plenty of examples from history and today that demonstrate the exploitation of religion and the abuse of power.

Human beings are imperfect and selfish, and people have misused or misrepresented religion and spirituality for power, money, propaganda, manipulation, ego, and selfish reasons and pleasure. This has been going on since the beginning of time, and hypocrisy and misconduct have tarnished many people's view of what spirituality means or what it has to offer.

Religion and spirituality can serve as an amazing gift in your life, but you must be able to decipher between the two to feel confident and grounded in your beliefs and discussions. For that reason, I want to highlight some of their differences. My hope is that this conversation clarifies your understanding and affirms what your heart already knows.

> *__Religion__ is organized by a group or community organization. It is an institutionalized system of attitudes, beliefs, and practices that are organized around the worship of God or the supernatural. Religious groups adopt a specific doctrine that defines its teachings. This is accepted by its members and may include a creed or outline of sacred prayers or rituals. Those who congregate under a particular faith are asked to abide by certain rules, laws, and a code of ethics. This provides order and structure and reinforces morality and benevolence. Of course, there are great variations in the organization of each religion.*

> *__Spirituality__ can stand alone. A person can be spiritual even if they don't identify with a particular religion. Spirituality is always grounded on two basic principles: the belief that there is a power greater than one's self and that human beings are called to experience some deeper transformation. It is an individual practice in which a person pursues some greater version of themselves. This is a personal journey in which a person explores their higher consciousness. They recognize that there is a divine association between their physical and emotional experiences. It is their connection to their own divinity that allows them to engage with people, nature, and animals on a profound*

level. When a person recognizes that everything is spiritual, they also understand that everyone is connected.

Learning about these differences is extremely beneficial to your life. It allows you to understand that people are on a sacred journey, and they are learning and growing at their own pace. This removes all expectations and judgments that people should be anywhere different from where they are.

Sure, it can be frustrating to witness people suffering, wasting their gifts, or spiraling out of control in their life, but people cannot be rushed or forced to grow. We evolve when we are ready and not a moment sooner. It also doesn't matter how bad we want it for someone else. They must be the one to initiate their healing and self-discovery.

As you know, adversity can take on many different forms. Death of a loved one, separation, divorce, illness, caregiving, or even an empty nest could thrust a person into massive change. These experiences are rarely prepared for, and they serve some transformative role in our lives. This is when you are invited to realign your energy, evaluate your priorities, address your emotional needs, and connect with your higher power.

Now, that's not exactly the first thing that we think about when shit hits the fan, or we experience some great loss. We tend to take it very personally and resist any notion that there could be some value to our pain. In fact, we tend to feel very much alone. However, grief is one of the great teachers in the world. It brings people together, and it humbles us. It teaches us the lesson that nothing on this earth belongs to us. Eventually, we shall release everything.

Spirituality affirms that we are never alone in our redemption, recovery, or mortality.

Faith in something greater than yourself may help you find peace in what is painful or unexplainable. Your human mind can only take you so far in your healing. Think about some of the harsh constructs of the world. We can't always explain **"WHY things happen."** Spirituality focuses on what is true and how we can bring forward love, healing, and self-improvement.

Now, that is vastly different from the way society deals with problems.

We sensationalize and overdramatize everything. We focus on misfortune instead of our growth.

"Did you hear what happened to me today?"

"Wait till you hear about the shit that unfolded at work yesterday!"

"You won't freaking believe this!"

Yes, all that drama may garnish a little attention at the moment, but it never makes you feel any better. It just reinforces chaos and the belief that you are a victim. You see, while the details of your trauma are very personal to you, they are not actually relevant to your healing. A lot of times, we get stuck on the details of what happened instead of addressing the emotions associated with adversity. It is the repetitive storytelling that delays your growth and healing.

As the information keeps running over and over in your brain, it causes rumination. This activates the **sympathetic response,** which places you in a state of emergency. So, what exactly does that look like?

These are the physiological changes that happen very quickly:

Your adrenal glands release hormones.

Your heart rate goes up.

Your breath is quick, short, and shallow.

Sweating occurs.

Blood moves to the muscles, leaving cold extremities.

Pupils dilate to see the threat better.

Digestion slows down because it's no longer a priority.

Can you imagine a car going full speed with no brakes? That's a good comparison of how the human body responds to fear, stress, and rumination. Eventually, the car will run out of gas or break down, and so do we. In choosing to take on a more spiritual approach, we are preserving our vehicle. In humans, our vessel includes the mind, body, and spirit, and it needs regular stops (rest), maintenance, and healing.

Spirituality not only has a positive effect on your thoughts but also restores balance throughout your body systems. Once you remove the noise and settle into some quiet state, you can engage the **parasympathetic response**, which deactivates the stress response and affirms feelings of wholeness, wellness, and safety. It untangles blocked energy where you can focus on physical, emotional, and spiritual nourishment and replenishment.

As you can see, these two patterns have very different vibrational frequencies. Rumination reinforces fear, anxiety, and survival, and spirituality reinforces calm energy and self-efficacy.

Anything that brings you turmoil needs your validation and healing, and the way that you do that is through spiritual analysis.

"What am I supposed to learn from this experience?"

"How does this experience help me to become a stronger human being?"

"How does this moment prepare me for the next level of life?"

If you notice, the question was NOT, **"Why did this happen TO me?"** Here is the simple reason for that. You can never reconstruct a physical moment in time. Anything that happens based on human interaction cannot be recreated, so you cannot understand other people's thoughts or motivations. Time will reveal answers and the changes that are supposed to happen. When you observe life from this spiritual lens, you shall see that life doesn't happen **TO** you ... It unfolds **FOR** you.

Here's a troubling reality. There are way too many people who are holding onto their pain from early childhood, and it's interfering with their present health and happiness. If this is true for you, it's likely that your parents or loved ones couldn't advocate for your emotional needs because they didn't have the capacity or toolbox to address their own traumas, worries, and fears. It's a dysfunctional cycle with no beginning or end unless you are willing to face the truth and your hurt feelings.

Here's what I would like to impress upon you. Generational pain isn't something that you can explain because it goes back way too far. If your loved ones were emotionally unavailable to you, it's because they were struggling with their own upbringing, confusion, dysfunction, or heartache. However, this is where you are empowered to break the cycle. You can cut the energetic cord, advocate for your own feelings, and consciously bring love forward. This is how you improve yourself and the generation to come.

You are not bound to pain, grief, or misery without your choice or permission. Perhaps you just need to simplify it another way. You may need to stop trying to figure out **"Why it happened."** If you choose to focus on the healing instead of the misfortune, you shall free yourself. Oh, and one more thing. Anything that you consider painful or disheartening is just God's invitation that you haven't gotten around to opening yet.

Stay Open.

Love,

Krista

Questions & Reflection

PART 1

Take a moment to think about what is most troubling to your heart. What is that invitation that you set aside a while ago because it was too difficult to deal with? Now, imagine how much energy it takes to ignore a part of yourself day after day. Use a page in your journal to write down what you now understand to be God's invitation. Once you identify what the issue is, write down any emotions that are associated with that experience. Let this be a free-flowing exercise. Do not edit your feelings. Whatever comes out on paper is perfect. When you are done, set it aside to come back to later.

PART 2[13]

I'm inviting you to do a meditation that allows you to tap into your Inner Guidance. This is that part of yourself that is aligned with your higher power. It is the voice within that guides you in times of grief, sorrow, or confusion. You may read the meditation aloud. However, the best scenario is to find a quiet place and listen to the words. You may tape your voice for this exercise or listen to the meditation link I have provided on my website.

When you enter this exercise, keep an open heart and open mind. Do not be attached to any specific outcome. Your inner guidance will clear energy that is no longer needed and facilitate the healing that supports your mind, body, and spirit. Your inner guidance already understands what you need for your highest and greatest good. Enjoy.

---

[13] This script has been adapted from my Mind-Body Medicine training. Some of the verbiage has been modified for this exercise. The goal is to connect with your spiritual guidance.

MEDITATION: Sit or lie down in a quiet place. Allow yourself to relax into a comfortable position. You may place your hands anywhere that feels comfortable to you: on your lap, by your side, across your belly, or over your heart. Now, take a slow breath in through your nose. Hold it for a few seconds, and then exhale fully. Push the air through your lips gently and allow any sounds to come forward.

Let's do that again. Take in a full breath through the nose. Hold it for a few seconds, then exhale until all the air is gone. Now, scan your body from the bottom of your feet to the top of your crown. Is there anything that you need at this moment to feel more comfortable? Feel free to make any adjustments. Once you are relaxed, you are welcome to close your eyes or find a soft gaze on the floor.

I invite you to imagine a beautiful place that brings you safety and comfort. It can be a space in your home or some lovely spot in nature. Maybe it's a place that you visited as a child, or perhaps it's somewhere you have never been to before. Allow your imagination to take you to the perfect place where you feel safe and cared for.

Take a moment to observe your surroundings. Allow your senses to take in everything peacefully. What do you notice? Are you around any trees or water? Do you hear any sounds in the background? Waves? Birds? Rustling leaves? How is the temperature? Is it warm, or is it cool? Do you feel the sun on you? Can you smell any fragrance?

Your higher self chose this place for you, and you are very peaceful here. Allow yourself to be curious. Do you feel in touch with your younger self? If so, what is your age? What kind of clothes are you wearing? Do you have shoes on, or are you barefoot? Do you have any favorite items with you? Consider for a moment what you would like to bring to this space to make you feel even more comfortable. You may do so now.

As you settle into this space, you become aware of something bustling in the distance. Something ethereal is moving toward you. You are not scared or threatened because you're already aware of its love and light. It is intended to serve as a sacred guide to help you through obstacles and challenges. How would you describe this force of good? Does it appear to be a woman, a man, a child, or perhaps an animal? Does it have a distinguishable essence or color? Can you get a feeling from this energy? If so, what is it?

You are very calm and welcoming. There is nothing to fear, as this energy represents another level of consciousness. It is here to support you, and it is aligned with your higher power. You are welcome to connect with this energy in any way that feels good. You might extend warm thoughts, kind words, or open arms. You may feel compelled to run toward this energy and offer a warm embrace. Whatever contact you decide to make is absolutely perfect.

This energy represents a divine source within you. It has love, guidance, and support to offer you whenever you need it. As you lean into this energy, you might ask your inner guidance if it has a message for you today. You can also ask a question or refer to the problem you wrote down in your envelope. You may ask for advice or a solution. Know that all answers are geared to help you to release fear, clear the energy centers in your body, and find peace within yourself. There is no wrong way to interact.

Once you have a message, thank your inner guidance for the support. You can tap into this energy whenever you need to. It just takes a safe place, a few quiet breaths, and your intention to reconnect with this energy. It will help clarify your needs and priorities and help you shift the energy if you feel stuck.

At this time, you can thank your inner guidance for support. As you release the image of your spiritual guide, know that you can engage with your guide whenever you need to. This is a part of your higher self, and it is designed to support you. At this moment, I invite you to take a big cleansing breath and slowly bring your awareness back to the room. When you are ready, you may open your eyes.

PART 3

The third part of this exercise is to write down what your experience was during the meditation. Describe your safe place and how it made you feel. Then, write down your observations on meeting your inner guide. What did your spiritual guide look like, and what message did it have for you? Was it a comfortable experience? Did you experience any challenges? What shifted for you? Write down any new revelations that came forward during the meditation to heal the burden you have been carrying. Upon completion of this exercise, take a moment to show love for yourself.

Feel free to do this exercise as many times as you desire. You are likely to have a different experience each time.

Chapter Eleven

The Day at Target

The fact that we have this inner guidance is very comforting. It means that God is never too far. It also means we don't have to rely on external things or other people to make us feel better. We have everything we need to calm ourselves and navigate through tough situations. The problem is that we're so used to holding in our feelings and masking our pain, we lose sight of how resilient we are.

There comes a point when pain culminates, and it cannot be contained any longer. The emotional dam will eventually break open, and you'll have to come to terms with your feelings whether you're ready or not. It happened to me. I had a little time between appointments, so I decided to pop into Target to look around. Sounds pretty normal and harmless, right? Well, there was nothing normal about it.

My family had just lost two parents within a few weeks of one another, the country was going through a pandemic and a tumultuous election, and protests and riots were breaking out all over the U.S. I wasn't conscious of how much pain and sadness I was absorbing. My oldest son had just left for college, and my youngest was locked up in his room for most of his senior year doing classes on Zoom.

I was holding on by a thread. It took just one strange interaction with a woman in Target for all that grief to come crashing in. I encountered her at the checkout lane. She said I was standing too close to her in line, and then she shamed me for allowing my mask to fall beneath my nostrils. She said, "It's been almost a year. You would think you would know how to put on a fu#%ing mask." I was absolutely appalled by her hostility, and I started shaking.

It was amazing how easy it was for her to belittle my existence. I quickly stood up for myself. "You don't even fu#%ing know me, and you're yelling at me." The scolding was completely uncalled for and triggered so many emotions in me that I lost it. I yelled right back at her, "I've had it! I'm done with you, and I'm done with all this Covid bullshit!" I yanked off my mask, threw down the $14 shirt that I was going to buy, and stormed out of Target.

Say what you will ... it wasn't my finest moment, but it went down that way. It was raw and ugly. Suddenly, I wasn't just mad at Covid and the girl who dumped all her fear over me. I was mad that we couldn't throw a proper funeral for Cathy and Dan, and I was mad that people were losing themselves! I went straight to my car and sobbed in the parking lot.

Grief, worry, anxiety, anger, and deep sadness poured down my face. I literally cried until I had no more tears left. I realized that grief had been building up for months. I never gave myself permission to feel the deep loss of my mother and father-in-law passing away. I also didn't realize how sad I felt about my older son moving away and how my younger son got jipped out his senior year.

I was so tired of people telling me to put on a stupid mask, and I was heartbroken about how sterile and nonsensical the world had become. There was this part of me that felt very small and powerless. That situation seemed to trigger other wounds that were inside me. I felt like a little girl who just wanted to curl up with her blanket.

I desperately wanted to go back to the way things were before Covid, but another part of me knew that Covid was taking us somewhere that we had never been before. It would challenge us to reconnect with our spirituality. My inner guidance fully understood that we weren't meant to go back, and our health and humanity depended on each person finding the courage to meet their fears during this very strange period of separation.

I had a bizarre conversation with myself and God on that day. I cussed and I ranted until there was nothing left to say. I finally talked myself into getting centered by taking a few Soft Belly Breaths. "C'mon girl, you learned this stuff in your mind-body medicine training. Now practice!" I closed my eyes and took three Soft Belly Breaths. Sure enough, the breathing brought me to a calm place.

I prayed and bargained with my angels to hold me up because I felt so exhausted. After several minutes of complete silence, I opened my eyes. Strangely, it felt like a different day. As I became aware of my physical surroundings again, I realized I had been in the Target parking lot for almost an hour.

I pulled the visor down and rubbed the black mascara from underneath my eyes. I started giving myself a pep talk. "Okay, Girl. Pull your shit together." I felt ready to restart my car and my life and put the entire experience behind me. Well, leave it to God to give me just what I needed.

As I turned on the ignition, the satellite radio popped on. There was some song playing that I had never heard before. The lyrics instructed to run until we find peace and it will set us free. I listened to every word. That song had perfect timing. It hugged me like an old friend.

I couldn't drive away. I had to keep listening to the guy with the raspy voice. His lyrics really hit home. It seemed that we both wanted to feel whole again and were tired of running and pretending. That song felt incredibly comforting. It was at that moment that I came to the realization that I had to fall apart and be with everything exactly as it was—messy and unfiltered. I needed to have that raw confrontation with my pain to make peace with it.

I felt so much relief to just let everything come out without any apology or explanation to anybody. I didn't have to put on a smile or be strong for anyone else. After months of holding everything together, I claimed my disappointment and sorrow. I had finally given myself permission to just sit with my grief and listen to what it wanted me to know.

That was a powerful moment! Something clicked inside me. I finally grasped the wisdom that I had no real control over the world or external pieces of my life where people come and go without saying goodbye. I couldn't change the fact that people get old or receive some diagnosis of cancer or dementia. I couldn't stop people from dying, I couldn't protect my children from getting hurt, nor could I control whether some girl in Target unleashed her anger on me. I only had the power to change one thing, and that was myself.

That day was a real game changer! It made me think about how common it is for us to pretend we aren't sad or hurt. Whether it relates back to the way we were raised or the social conditioning, most people are taught early in life to hide, control, or withhold their feelings so it doesn't make anyone else feel uncomfortable. **"Stop crying! Be polite! Don't be a baby! Real men don't cry! You're too sensitive! You stop those tears, or I will give you something to cry about!"**

It's true society has imposed strange rules and cruel stereotypes on us for simply being vulnerable. Men are labeled soft and weak when they show emotions or tears, and women are considered overly dramatic if they get weepy. The whole thing makes me rather curious. Why does expressing sadness or frailty make us feel like we've done something wrong? Who decided that it's impolite or offensive? I now find myself questioning those narratives. It seems to me that feeling is the only real bridge to healing.

Learning to be with grief and sadness has to be one of the bravest things that we can ever do. It literally saves us so much time and energy that we can be investing into our relationships, growth, and joy. It's freedom, and it allows us to meet our greatest human potential. It's a lot of pressure to keep hiding or piling our emotions on top of one another, and here's the truth of it all—if we aren't able to honor the feelings that are inside of us, then we shall spend the bulk of our life hiding who we truly are.

Sadly, that strange vacancy inside us cannot be filled by anything but our own love and acceptance. Part of the reason I decided to share the Target story is because it's so darn relatable ... the angry girl, the $14 shirt, and the messy cry in the parking lot. It all brings a certain humanness to this conversation. We can be going about our day minding our own business. Then, BAM! There it is! The Universe gives us an opportunity to confront our pain, and we can either ignore it or hide it in a new place.

If you were conditioned to believe that vulnerability is a sign of weakness, you're likely to bury your pain over and over. There may be several experiences in your history where you were taught to suck up your feelings and be a good little girl/boy. Now, those messages could have been verbalized or reinforced through various unspoken behaviors.

Imagine the child who starts crying, and the parent's response is to give them a cookie or a toy, or place them in front of the TV. Without realizing it, the child learns that their feelings are not okay and they need to be comforted by food, entertainment, or some other distraction. These are the kinds of moments that shape our emotional habits.

It sets up a scary precedent in which we advance those patterns to our adult behavior. Instead of coping with our sadness, we might adopt some dysfunctional habits like binging on food or TV, alcoholism, pot smoking, hoarding, shopping, etc. It's interesting how a precedent is set early in our lives. If we grow up believing that we shouldn't express our tears or sadness, then that coping system just continues.

This feels like the perfect moment to ask you to review your family history.

- **What kind of early messages were you given about expressing your emotions?**

- **Were you encouraged to speak up and talk about your feelings?**

- **Were you reprimanded for expressing tears or sadness?**

- **Were there unspoken rules to abide by in which you learned to be quiet and just deal with your sadness on your own?**

These questions may unlock some answers for you. Reviewing your family history is a great way to develop some personal insight because it's relevant to your current mindset, emotional habits, and physical well-being. There are way too many people in this world who have developed stress-related health problems and psychosomatic disorders (illnesses that seemingly have no known physical cause) as a result of holding in their pain and holding back their emotions.

It's amazing how the body responds to stress over time. It pleads with us to slow down, and sadly, most of us don't listen until we are dealt with some illness or diagnosis. All of this represents the relationship between the mind, body, and spirit. Everything is interconnected. If any part of that dynamic is out of alignment, then the other areas will suffer.

At this moment, you have permission to script out an entirely different message for yourself if it is needed. Perhaps, after all these years, you have been subconsciously waiting for some sort of permission to have your emotions. Well, that permission can come right now from you.

What if all those emotions that you have learned to hide aren't looking for anything but your acknowledgment? We've overcomplicated our healing. There's so much power in owning our feelings. It doesn't have to be a big production or dramatic performance. It can be something as simple as:

"I feel sad."

"I feel disappointed."

"I feel a little lost right now."

"I feel lonely."

"I feel confused."

"I feel angry."

"I feel heartbroken."

"I feel …"

That day at Target taught me a profound lesson. I need to own my feelings as I go through my experiences; no more stockpiling!

In giving myself permission to have my emotions, I also give others permission to have theirs too.

So, let me bring you back to that moment in the car. The song on the radio was slowly coming to an end. I decided to pull up the information on the satellite radio to see what the name of it was. It was called **"Redemption"** by Daniel Radcliffe. I immediately thought of Cathy and knew that it was a sign from her to surrender my pain to God and give myself Grace.

I took hold of the blessing happening in that parking lot and decided to stop feeling sorry for myself. I came to the conclusion that it was time to stop pretending that I wasn't sad. I wasn't some victim of circumstance. God was just teaching me a few lessons about human frailty, letting go of things that I have no control over, self-compassion, and accepting the impermanence of life.

Everyone has some **"Story of Redemption."** The details may differ, but it does require several brave decisions.

- You commit to moving forward.

- You reserve the right to honor your truth.

- You acknowledge how you feel.

- You face your greatest fear.

- You turn your painful experience over to your higher power.

I'll be the first one to tell you that it's not easy, but like anything else, the more practice you give to the process, the easier it is to form new habits. Redemption is the return of self, and what we must remember is that there is nothing too big or too small that you and the Universe can't handle together. In the end, it will set you free.

Stay Vulnerable.

Love,

Krista

Questions & Reflection

1) When you look back at your family history, what messages were you given about expressing your feelings? **Feel free to elaborate. Were you encouraged to express your feelings freely, or were you reprimanded or instructed to deal with your emotions quietly?**

2) Can you cite a moment in your life when you were directly or indirectly told to keep your feelings to yourself? **(This could be from any time period of your life.)**

3) Identify a difficult situation in your life in which you had a hard time coming to terms with your sadness, grief, or other difficult emotions.

   What is that feeling that you pushed down?

4) Please finish the following sentence. **Today, I give myself permission to feel ...**

Chapter Twelve

Tangled

*E*very chapter in this book takes you one step closer to knowing yourself on a much deeper level and appreciating the role of emotions. My hope is that you are able to see yourself through a more compassionate lens. Many of us have unconsciously created barriers to loving ourselves because we have taken on the expectations and judgments of others or we have imposed the rigid standard of perfection on ourselves.

It's unrealistic to believe that everything will go your way all the time. There's no promise that life will be easy or guarantee you won't go through periods of grief, confusion, or suffering. Suffering is a lonely and isolating experience because the person believes they are stuck, and they lose hope in themselves and everything around them.

Trauma isn't something that you can necessarily prepare for. It can come on like a mad truck and cause long bouts of pain if you don't get underneath it. That's why it's important to understand how your spirituality can assist you through difficult changes in your life and comfort you so that you never feel alone.

Suffering is the slow deterioration of self. It interferes with your state of mind, energy, physical and emotional well-being, and your overall spirit. It's difficult to pinpoint the exact problem because your energy gets tangled into one impossible knot, and somewhere in this unbearable situation is the REAL you.

The person suffering may not have the words to express what they need or what is missing. They just know that they cannot go on living this way. One could associate suffering with a significant loss, a devastating event, a crisis, an abusive relationship, or a toxic person. It can relate to depression, a medical condition, or a painful childhood. It's anything that is unresolved and stews over time.

People who feel stuck in their turmoil feel disconnected from their spirituality, and they long to be saved. Suffering could be a temporary state, or it could represent a lifetime of heartache. Unless there's some intervention, it will intensify and jeopardize a person's health, relationships, and aspirations.

Many people who let pain overstay its welcome fall victim to depression, isolation, or addictions. In extreme cases, some people will literally abandon their life completely. They might tell themselves that they don't want to risk further injury, but they're just avoiding the healing process because it's too painful. Their self-worth is lost, and they don't believe that anyone could possibly show up for them. Sadly, they don't know how to show up for themselves either.

Suffering is not just the deterioration of self but the loss of hope in trusted resources: family, friends, doctors, teachers, law enforcement, humanity, and even God. When fear drives a person's life, they feel unsafe and unsupported. This translates to insecurity, and it subconsciously affects every major decision in their life.

Part of your higher education is understanding how to tap into your spiritual support and resilience so that you can manage disappointment, fear, conflict, sadness, anger, grief, and disparity. If you confront your emotional discomfort right away and allow your spirituality to have space in this process, then you can untangle the experience from yourself and graduate to the next level of consciousness.

This untangling doesn't mean that you have to repair or remove the experience from your life story. Instead, you work with it and allow it to take its rightful place in your journey. From the beginning of time, human beings have suffered mentally, emotionally, and physically. Generations before us have battled oppressive regimes, evil, devastating elements, natural disasters, illness, disease, famine, dehydration … the list goes on and on. While those things posed huge threats to our physical survival, I will go out on a limb and say that today's greatest challenge is **"spiritual suffering."**

Spiritual suffering is when we deny the relationship to the divine and the need for love, faith, hope, virtue, and beauty. In disregarding our connection to our higher power, inner guidance, and to one another, we become deeply troubled and feel like our life is meaningless.

I read an article not too long ago. It was from OFS Health Care, in which a nun named Sister Jacque Schroeder, who worked in palliative care, described her findings of spiritual suffering.

She said, **"Spiritual pain is the pain that comes from the hidden areas of our life. It can't be pointed to on a pain scale, but it is still very real and can impact our physical and emotional health."**

Sister Jacque Schroeder went on to describe the different categories of spiritual pain.

- **MEANING**—struggling with the "meaning" behind life, relationships, and the world around you

- **FORGIVENESS**—pain that stems from forgiving others, ourselves, and God

- **RELATEDNESS**—dealing with relationships, whether good or bad

- **HOPE**—feeling like there is no hope or it doesn't exist

Her explanation was simple. **"We cannot fix what we do not acknowledge. Spiritual pain doesn't discriminate based on gender or age; it affects everyone in different ways at all stages of life. Everyone is on a spiritual journey from the moment they are born, and from that journey, we feel pain and, in turn, we grow. Our society doesn't often emphasize this journey, so we have a difficult time dealing with the pain when it becomes too much to handle."** [14]

It seems that the older I get, the more suffering I witness in this world. Whether it's the older generation that is dealing with health ailments and coming to terms with mortality or the younger generation who is managing so much fear and struggling to find their identity and sense of purpose, there's a clear increase in anxiety, depression, and mental health problems.

So what is it about today's world that we feel so overwhelmed, fearful, defeated, and heart-sick, and why is there an escalation in spiritual suffering? Well, let's see if we can break this question down into smaller pieces. Let's explore this further and consider

---

[14] Michael Vujovich, "Understanding Spiritual Pain: OSF Healthcare," OSF HealthCare Blog, February 10, 2022, https://www.osfhealthcare.org/blog/understanding-spiritual-pain/.

how this applies to your life. You are welcome to pull out your journal and write down your thoughts. There are no right or wrong answers. Just allow whatever ideas and opinions that you have to come through.

- **Is there anything in your belief system that prevents you from acknowledging your spiritual pain?**

- **Historically, human suffering has a way of waking people up in such a way that they look inward for compassionate answers. What do we need more of in this world?**

- **There is a personal cost in managing pain all on your own. What has that been like for you?**

- **What can you do to further educate yourself about spirituality? Is there a local bookstore, are there classes or workshops you can take in person or online, or is there a group or congregation you can tap into for support? Write down some ideas to follow up on.**

Resilience is an extension of faith, so the only answer that makes sense for any of these questions is to take a deeper look at your own spirituality. I would like to believe that we embark on our spiritual journey because we love ourselves and God so much, but self-care may not be the driving force. The more likely scenario is that we go through a devastating experience and feel utter despair. I find it is no coincidence that certain life experiences will bring you to your knees. It's a call for more reverence, prayer, and self-reflection.

Without adversity or the struggle of human suffering, we wouldn't understand the value of life or appreciate the little things that bring us fulfillment or comfort. We need contrast to give us perspective. Whether it's physical light and darkness or the experience of joy and pain, God's presence can be felt in seasons, nature, the never-ending cycle of daytime and nighttime, and the human condition.

Once you understand that you need not be perfect to experience unconditional love and acceptance, the need to hide, pretend, or skip through the uncomfortable experiences slowly goes away. Spirituality grants you the wisdom to take care of yourself regardless of where you are in your life. It's ironic how human frailty mirrors spiritual frailty; this is why many people experience an awakening during times of suffering.

Despite all your wonderful efforts, you're not perfect or impervious to mistakes or wrongdoing. You are not fully protected from getting hurt, sick, or even dying. All these painful experiences take you to the next level of expansion, where you are aligned with your heart, faith, and virtues.

Once you make spirituality a part of your life, several beautiful changes occur:

- **You stop picking yourself apart or comparing yourself to others.**

- **You give yourself permission to have your emotions.**

- **You release the fear of judgment and other people's opinions of you.**

- **You trust the time and order of things happening in your life.**

- You learn to trust your higher power and inner guidance.

- You replace self-criticism with self-love.

- You learn to love others where they are in their journey.

- You accept the impermanence of life.

Sister Jacque Schroeder felt that the remedy for spiritual pain was very simple. She said it's "silence and breathing." That means that we consciously turn down the noise in our lives so we can receive spiritual messages and digest life lessons. Of course, the only problem with her recommendation is that most people can't sit still, put their phones down, or be quiet long enough to reflect.

In today's society, we are more likely to look outside ourselves for answers than to connect with spirituality. However, when we accept other people's opinions, judgments, and assessments of ourselves and the world, we stop listening to our inner guidance. We stop listening to our heart and intuition. It is critical to our physical well-being and happiness that we take time for self-analysis and ask ourselves deeper questions about what we need to be lighter in terms of worry, stronger in the way of resilience, and more compassionate for ourselves and others.

This is the essence of "soul searching." You intentionally pause and breathe. Then, you engage in some personal inventory of your life. With stillness, you can invoke the love and support of your higher power, and then you listen to your internal advice. Sadly, our greatest problem as a society is that we have strayed away from this very intuitive process. If we take on the loudest voice in the room, we surrender our safety and peace of mind to others. We literally stop thinking for ourselves and advocating for our well-being and the things we care about. This is how dependencies are born.

After years of listening to the news, reading magazines, following social media trends, and adhering to pressure and societal norms, human beings have bought into an extreme habit. We constantly label ourselves, other people, and our experiences as either **"GOOD or BAD."** This has placed us in a very precarious position. We see things in life as fair or unfair, just or unjust, and right or wrong. It polarizes us into groups of The Haves and Have-NOTS ... the privileged and the victims.

Right now, we are seeing this play out politically and socially. You can see how this labeling has set us back in our healing because it promotes fear, separation, and survival. Here's the larger problem ... by turning over our beliefs, power, and individuality to others, we stop holding ourselves accountable for happiness, our choices, and the state of the world. Everything is just somebody else's fault.

It's a strange time in the world because we're not just looking to help ourselves; we need to find our soul again as a human collective. There are a lot of broken systems that have been overrun by personal interests and corruption. We're not going to be able to fix them overnight. You could literally combine the knowledge and expertise of political scientists, economists, infectious disease specialists, environmentalists, judicial specialists, humanitarians, social workers, doctors, and teachers and still come up short in healing the world.

It's not due to a shortage of knowledge or ideas that hold us back from peace. It's because there is a lack of selflessness and love. This is why spirituality is the only unifying answer. It gives us sensibility, compassion for every person on the planet, and, most importantly, personal accountability. **Spirituality serves as a moral** guidepost for which we make decisions that are for the highest good of all. Without it, humans fall victim to their egos, greed, selfishness, and the desire for self-importance.

Energy is continuously moving through us. Love, pain, joy, money, relationships, and even death represent different forms of energy coming and going from our lives, but we have no real proof that anything is good or bad. We won't understand its true purpose until we take time for introspection.

Spirituality clarifies our human experiences and our greater reason for being here, and without that foundation, a person will not be invested in themselves, humanity, or the care of the planet. We may not realize it, but by telling ourselves that some part of our story is **"Bad,"** we subconsciously undermine our own value and purpose for being. This informs the Universe that we aren't open to receiving new blessings.

The label "Bad" may serve a certain protection in our lives, but it doesn't help us heal or grow any faster. It creates a barrier to peace, abundance, wellness, kind experiences, or loving relationships. Most of us aren't even aware of how this label reduces our value and diminishes the worth of other human beings.

Here are a few examples in which we isolate something uncomfortable, judge it, and label it, but we haven't done the self-reflection or analysis to understand its greater purpose.

> *"I had a bad childhood."*

> *"That was a bad time in my life."*

> *"My health is bad."*

> *"I'm in the middle of a bad divorce."*

"I have a bad relationship with_____."

"I have a bad feeling about this."

"The world is in a bad place."

"It's bad news."

Everything is subjective. When we label something "Bad" we are warning ourselves and others to stay away from that situation or person. However, none of those statements bring any kind of understanding, resolution, or acceptance, so whatever lesson or wisdom we are supposed to take away from the experience remains lost.

We tend to use the term "Bad" because we haven't taken the time to sort through the confusion or pain yet. Our energy is still tangled up in shock, sadness, disillusionment, or fear. This may be the case for a person who hasn't dealt with childhood pain, abandonment, neglect, trauma, or the death of a loved one.

This is the kind of self-care that is missing from our lives. We aren't taking the extra steps to process our emotions. When we postpone our grief for too long, we no longer know what to call it or what to do with it. This massive entanglement may seem like it has no beginning and no end.

So, how do you address that inner conflict that has made a home in your mind, body, and spirit?

Well, as Sister Jacque Schoeder stated, you begin with breath and silence. From there, you engage your spirituality and curiosity. This is an inquiry of your higher self. It is intended to raise your self-awareness. It's true you cannot reverse time or pain, but you can acknowledge its presence, get in touch with what you feel, and take away wisdom.

"How do I feel about this experience?"

"What is this situation prompting me to do?"

"How will I change as a result of going through this difficult experience?"

"How can this experience make me a better person?"

These questions represent the inner work needed to process hard things in your human journey.

You can't experience peace or redemption as long as your energy is tangled and tethered to something throbbing and aching. Only you know what that wound is in your story, and only you can go inward to administer love.

While I have a lot more to say about how to untangle these knots, I want to take Sister Jacque's advice and stop. Take a little time to breathe and sit in silence. Allow this chapter to settle into the space that it needs to. You already know what needs to be healed.

Stay Grounded.

Love,

Krista

Personal Reflection

Take time to sit in silence and do soft belly breathing. Take note of anything in your life that presents a conflict, problem, or issue. At this moment, you do not need to do anything with this tangled energy; just notice how you feel.

Chapter Thirteen

Untangling the Knots

I want to ask you to consider how pain affects your body, your thoughts, your energy, and your aspirations over time. If you set up a pattern of avoidance in your life, deny your truth, or withhold your grief or sadness, it will slowly deplete you physically, emotionally, mentally, and spiritually.

Fear can take over and override your other vital processes like your immune system (protection against pathogens and infectious disease), limbic system (behavioral and emotional responses), nervous system (sensation and motor responses), and intuition (instinct, awareness, creativity, imagination, insight, and holistic thoughts).

When you set aside purposeful time for reflection, you not only create a safe space to acknowledge your emotions, but you can tap into your higher guidance for direction. This is an important step to healing because you can clarify your values and priorities and decide what actions are needed to untangle the negative energy from your life.

Remember, not all situations are meant to be fixed or repaired. We just need to take the wisdom that we have learned from the experience and release the rest. We may think that apologies are needed to fully let go, but the forgiveness we wait for may not have anything to do with another person. It might be self-for-giveness or releasing our own expectations and attachments.

Healing looks easy on paper, but it's very challenging when you insert the details of your own story, particularly if you have experienced abandonment; the death of a loved one; physical, emotional, or sexual abuse; trauma; separation; or divorce. Until you own that thing in your life that is **"Bad,"** it quietly sits in the background, pulling energy away from your life and depleting your spirit.

You may subconsciously avoid a situation because you think that there's nothing you can do to change the outcome or repair broken trust. You might also tell yourself that you won't put yourself in a position to be hurt ever again. This is when you face a decision. The fork in the road is split between self-protection and healing. Survival prolongs the pain, but the spiritual path frees you from your burdens. **In every case of spiritual suffering, peace is not about the "undoing" but coming to terms with the truth and allowing space for self-compassion.**

When you are attached to a different outcome, you experience suffering. By simply acknowledging to yourself and God that some part of your energy is still tangled up with another person or a painful experience, you can begin the healing process. The slightest shift in your attitude can help you see things more clearly.

- **Release the false notion of perfection that you have imposed onto yourself. Pain, mistakes, and failures are all part of this human journey.** You are not the exception.

- **Release all attachments that you have for another person to act a certain way or live their life differently.** Acknowledge that you do not have control over how other people behave, make choices, or carry out their lives. Everybody has their own free will and individual journey.

- **Release the burden to fix, solve, and repair everything that is broken or painful.** It is not your responsibility to impose yourself on situations that do not belong to you. Some things may belong to other people; other things may belong to God. Nevertheless, they are out of your control, and they aren't meant to be fixed by you. Some experiences or problems may simply show up to present a lesson for you, another human being, or humanity.

- **Release the narrative that you are all alone in this journey.** At no point are you without love, support, or guidance, but it relies on you surrendering your ego and control and asking for support from your higher power.

- **Release the notion that things are either "Good or Bad."** When you release these extremes, you can see new possibilities.

This brings up a joyful memory for me. I remember going to dinner at my in-law's place a few years back. My mother-in-law, Catherine, always showed up to the community dining room with something to share. Sometimes, it was a bottle of wine. Other times, it was a good story. On that particular night, she recited a parable. She said that she heard it on the radio and was moved by the simplicity of the story. She sipped her glass of rosé and then delightfully shared.

> There is a Taoist story of an old farmer who had worked his crops for many years. One day, his horse ran away. Upon hearing the news, his neighbors came to visit. "Such bad luck," they said sympathetically.

"Maybe," the farmer replied.

The next morning, the horse returned, bringing with it three other wild horses. "How wonderful," the neighbors exclaimed.

"Maybe," replied the old man.

The following day, his son tried to ride one of the untamed horses, was thrown, and broke his leg. The neighbors again came to offer their sympathy for what they called his "misfortune."

"Maybe," answered the farmer.

The day after, military officials came to the village to draft young men into the army. Seeing that the son's leg was broken, they passed him by. The neighbors congratulated the farmer on how well things had turned out.

"Maybe," said the farmer.

Years later, I still recall the story and the kind wisdom of my mother-in-law. I have since learned that the story dates back to the 2nd century B.C., and Catherine was behind a long list of famous philosophers who used that tale to teach students and loved ones about the mysteries of fortune and suffering. What we perceive to be "Good, Bad ... Right or Wrong" is just a perception. Should you choose to be in a place of "Maybe" then you shall leave the space open for new possibilities and perspectives.

If you were to think back to a situation where someone came and left your life rather abruptly, you might think of it as a "bad experience." However, time and reflection will often reveal something transformative. These people who appear to be antagonists may actually be taking you through some necessary lessons that will teach you about boundaries and self-love.

Of course, there are plenty of moments when people go through their trials, mistakes, and obstacles, but they don't seek any responsibility or lesson. I'm pretty sure we have all been on the receiving end of a friend or loved one who complains about something stressful or painful in their life, but they never do anything about it. They whine, rant, protest, and dump their entire story all over you, and when they're done, they feel better, but now you feel terrible. Sadly, that is the extent of their emotional work.

When people complain, they may feel slightly better to get that weight off their shoulders, but they also skip the most important part. They miss the opportunity to take responsibility for themselves, improve their character, or elevate their consciousness. However challenging a problem may initially appear, you can shift it to love, forgiveness, peace, or even gratitude if you choose to do so.

Think of these situations as knots, and they represent the tangled energy that has yet to be resolved. I have noticed that not everyone uses the word "Bad," so I want to invite you to think about how you characterize things that are upsetting. I can think of a number of phrases that we assign to situations that are stressful, painful, unfair, or disturbing.

"This sucks!"

"This is terrible!"

"This is ridiculous!"

"This is unbelievably hard!"

"This is a complete shitshow!"

"This is overwhelming!"

"This is NOT fair!"

Hang in there with me because this is the important part! **When we tell ourselves that something in our lives is not okay, then we are in some way reinforcing that we aren't okay either.** We are in judgment of ourselves. Therefore, we are rejecting our ability to self-manage and persevere. This leaves us feeling weak, uneasy, unworthy, and unorganized. This not only affects us emotionally, physically, and psychologically, but it creates energetic blocks in our bodies, and this impedes our healing.

I came up with the acronym **"KNOTS"** as a way to make it easier for you to lean on your spirituality. This is a simple way to envision how your energy can get tangled and attached to unexpressed pain, unhealthy relationships, or unresolved grief. The acronym reinforces spiritual concepts that allow you to get in touch with your resilience.

Knots do not untangle themselves. They take patience and intention. If you trust your higher self to take you through a tangled experience, you will get to the other side of your grief, trauma, fear, or whatever ails your heart.

K = Keep patience and curiosity.

Something uncomfortable is happening. This is the time to bring in patience. Ask yourself, "What is the lesson unfolding for me right now?" Leave space for new possibilities and blessings.

N = Not everything is understood at the moment.

Place your trust that something may be happening FOR YOU instead of TO YOU!

You cannot heal or move forward if you are attached to being a victim.

O = Own your emotions.

Give yourself permission to feel. Do so without any judgment or concern about pleasing others. Just be REAL with yourself.

T = Take this moment as an invitation to go inward.

This is an opportunity to reframe your experience and bring in self-compassion. You may want to call on your inner guidance for courage and direction.

S = Stay open and present.

This is the time to breathe. With just a few breaths, you can find your quiet place. This is how you dial back the stress, calm your nervous system, and reconnect with your safety and inner peace. Presence is necessary for your healing. If your thoughts are attached to the past or caught up in fear, call your energy back to the present moment, where you are safe.

As you move through this book, you're starting to see that patience and self-compassion are necessary for your healing. It's never too late to untangle a knot or bring in your faith. In the end, it's best not to postpone your joy for something you can shift right now. Those knots won't untangle themselves.

Stay Patient.

Love,

Krista

Questions & Reflection

I want to come back to the concept of **"Good or Bad."** Is there something or someone in your life right now or in your past that you have characterized as **"Bad?"** This is a great time to pull out your journal. You may free-write, or you can address the questions below.

"What experience still has the aura of "Bad" that has been buried away?"

"How do I currently feel about this experience?"

"What emotions am I in touch with?"

"Is there something I can release to make this experience lighter?"

"Is there an action I can take to improve this situation?"

"Has a relationship with someone run its course?"

"How have I changed as a result of going through this difficult experience?"

"How does this experience make me a better person?"

"What advice does my inner guidance have for me?"

Chapter Fourteen

Lean in!

*I*t wasn't too long ago that my husband bought a golf cart. He was so excited to take me for a ride in it. Well, when you ride one of these carts, you don't put on a typical seatbelt. You just grab onto the handlebar. He drove alongside regular cars on the open road, he swerved in and out of neighborhoods, and when we got to the golf course, he drove across the bumpy greens, causing my entire body to bounce up and down.

I looked over at him from time to time, and I noticed that he was having the time of his life, but I felt like I was holding on for dear life. Now, I'm sure that sounds a little dramatic, but I couldn't stand that we weren't traveling on a designated path, or at least the one that I perceived to be safe. I can remember him looking over at me, recognizing my fear, and advising me, **"You're not having fun because you are holding on so tight. Relax your body and lean into the turns!"**

I share that story because, for most of my life, I've held onto everything pretty tightly—relationships, expectations, old habits. It's funny how certain behaviors start at a very young age and carry over into adulthood. Bracing myself wasn't anything new. I've been doing that since I was a little girl.

It may be a strange comparison, but when Paul said, "Lean into the turns," I had this epiphany that God was asking me to do the same thing: to trust him and lean into the experiences that are scary, upsetting, and otherwise out of my control. As soon as I got home, I picked up my laptop and immediately started writing about the concept of **"leaning in."**

As human beings, we like to believe that we are in charge of the things coming and going from our lives. We like to know where we are going and how we will get there. The only trouble with that is that we cannot prepare for everything. Life shows us time and time again that unexpected changes happen, and we are not the ones in charge. For that reason, there is no real mastery of life. The only thing promised is this never-ending invitation to know yourself and God a little bit better.

Your life becomes your own when you have the courage to step into the unknown. Whether it's your gifts, talent, power, heart, creativity, growth, education, healing, faith, intuition, curiosity, growth, or sense of adventure, all magical possibilities can only be uncovered by one person ... and that is YOU! There is no passage too big or too difficult when you align with God.

Unless you are willing to go deeper in your self-discovery, you shall remain tightly wrapped and tethered to other people's lives, opinions, and expectations. I can assure you from my own experience that you won't have very much fun because instead of doing things from your heart, you will do things out of pressure, guilt, and obligation. It's a lonely place because you believe your happiness is tied to giving, helping, and pleasing people.

Only you can unlock the magic and wisdom within your soul, but it requires some trust that God will help you navigate through moments when you feel like you have lost control. **"Lean in"** signifies courage. It is a mindset in which you accept your role as a co-creator. To lean in is to choose yourself and faith over and over again.

It's certainly easier to lean into joyful things, but it's crucial to your health to lean into the hard shit too. When you lean into the things that hurt, scare, offend, overwhelm, or irritate you, new perspectives and guidance become available. When you admit to yourself that you may not have all the answers, you can let go of your fear, sadness, and confusion.

So much of the stress we carry relates to our emotional habits. Some of those habits are difficult to break because they trace back to early childhood. If you lived through dysfunctional situations that made you feel unsafe, then you may have a hard time trusting that your needs will be met. If you dealt with separation or neglect, then you may have a fear of abandonment. If you were told that you weren't good enough, smart enough, or thin enough, then you are likely to question whether you deserve good things.

Avoiding vulnerability doesn't protect us from getting hurt because we are closing ourselves off to everything else: love, spiritual guidance, and new perspectives that could enlighten us. Resistance prolongs grief and reinforces fear and insecurity. In fact, it's likely to set up a whole new set of problems like sickness, depression, or extreme habits. Yes, whatever false notion of control that we think we have over grief is an illusion on our part.

The longer we keep the turmoil inside, the more we identify with it. Pain is a separate experience that is meant to move through us. It's when we try to hold it, control it, or smother it that we can no longer decipher what it means to our life or how it can possibly help us evolve to the next level of consciousness.

It's important to express what we feel, but if complaining about our problems is the extent of our emotional work, we just give pain a home by reinforcing it within ourselves. There is a very big difference between saying, **"I am sad,"** and **"I feel sad."** One is here to stay; the other is just passing through. It's important to frame our emotions in such a way that we give ourselves permission to shift the energy from fear to love.

So, what are some other phrases that people say out loud that can reinforce more tension and stress?

"I am mad!"

"I am stressed!"

"I am pissed off!"

"I am so angry!"

"I am afraid."

"I am horrified!"

"I am depressed!"

"I am devastated!"

"I am scared!"

"I am worried!"

"I am heartbroken!"

"I am overwhelmed!"

By the way, I have said all of those things out loud, but once I learned that pain is a messenger, I became self-aware of how I was encouraging more drama in my life and more stress in my mind and body. We can feel any and all of those emotions, but we must see pain as a temporary guest. The truth is, we have no idea how our experiences will transform us in purposeful ways or nudge us toward something more loving or supportive.

If you allow pain to overstay its welcome, it will drain you and prevent you from accessing those higher vibrational emotions **(Love, Joy, Equanimity, Wonder, Forgiveness, Compassion, Awe, and Gratitude).** These are the spiritual emotions that elevate your human experience and steer you toward love and healing.

As a society, we have done a poor job of teaching this generation how to deal with their emotions, anxiety, and stress, and it has had damaging effects on their well-being and psyche. Consider the impact of the pandemic. Aside from losing in-person instruction, social interaction, and extracurricular activities, most teens lost joy, self-confidence, and excitement for the future.

It's startling to think about the level of stress and pressure that this younger generation feels, but it doesn't necessarily end with them. People of all ages are still rattled by the experience, and it's because they never addressed their feelings or fears. When something monumental like Covid brings the entire world to a stop, we are supposed to pause and reflect on how it changes us for better or for worse. However, because many people avoided this process, they missed the opportunity to grow and connect with their faith.

It's true many people abandoned themselves during that time because they felt powerless. They clung to fear instead of their spirituality. The sad part of that Covid story is realizing that we are about five minutes from falling into that same trauma unless we take the time to evaluate what was lost. If you ask me, God is begging us to slow down and get in touch with our priorities again.

If we can get honest with ourselves about what we feel, then we can determine what the larger lessons are for us individually and as a society. It takes courage to find Grace. It's that **"digging in"** that allows a person or a society to recover, emotionally progress, build immunity, and become resilient. Unless we embrace the truth of where we have been, we are likely to replicate the same traumas in the future.

Do you ever wonder why we aren't addressing our emotional problems? Does it bother you that we can't get a handle on universal interests like public health and safety? Does it alarm you that society seems to be turning a blind eye to social unrest, a mental health crisis, violence, homelessness, drug addiction, and other horrific traumas? Why aren't we coming together to collaborate on problems that are fully within our control? What are we waiting for?

Sadly, it's more profitable to talk about pandemics, war, conflict, trauma, sickness, tragedy, anxiety, physical ailments, and separation than to talk about peace, love, and healing. Right now, control and dominance are more important than your current well-being and happiness, and fear-mongering is just a tactic used to achieve power and create some hierarchy. This is why your journey to find Grace and inner peace will be one of the most courageous things that you can do for yourself.

With widespread chaos and distractions imposing larger inter-FEAR-ence on your health and harmony, you must be the one to insist on self-love, wellness, and consciousness. You do so by creating a support system for yourself which allows you to explore your divinity. This could be your family, a church, a spiritual group, or a circle of friends that empower you to grow beyond your current limits to become the healthiest version of yourself.

When you permit yourself to explore your spirituality and healing, you will generate ripples of love and goodness all around you. Sure, there will be moments when you feel like you're swimming upstream, but that's because you're confronting fears, breaking cycles, and releasing the pain of previous generations.

When you open yourself to spirituality, you conspire with the Universe to achieve another level of balance, love, peace, and fulfillment. Your path is not going to look like anything you've ever seen before. You just have to lean in and establish that trust that informs God that you are open to receiving your abundance.

In some strange irony, this is the very reason that society dismisses spirituality. God interferes with private agendas. You see, the less spiritual we are, the weaker we are. The more fearful we are, the easier it is to manipulate us to think a certain way. This sets a dangerous precedent where people stop listening to their intuition and inner guidance, and then they are more likely to lose their confidence and independence. Society wants us to fall in line and be compliant, but God wants us to be free thinkers, innovators, and healers.

Imagine what it's like to be a young person in today's world. Kids aren't allowed to be kids anymore. They are dealing with too many harsh realities: drugs, war, gender identity, depression, political separation, protests, not feeling safe on the streets, and not being able to afford to buy a home. Yes, they have so much to worry about, and as a result, they have tempered their dreams and aspirations. They are cautious not to get overly excited about the future because they have little confidence in the world to support or keep them safe.

That's not the kind of world that I have imagined for my sons. Becoming better means that we have the courage to review our emotions and experiences, our choices, and our mistakes. This is why we aren't meant to erase history. We must learn from it so that we don't repeat problems. Understanding where we came from may be more important than we once understood. It gives us a higher bar to improve ourselves and humanity.

Just as you and I are looking for greater answers to today's problems, so are a million other souls, and I find that inspiring! Of course, none of this is easy. We are susceptible to all the fear campaigns that are fed to us by news agencies and political leaders, but this is precisely why you need to dial into Grace. It's your own positive channel and advice center. It's already in you, and it's a breath of fresh air for today's world.

We are dealing with conflicting messages all the time, so how do we know if something is working for our highest good or depleting us? Well, you can come back to this question to discover the answer, **"Does this experience, person, or energy feed fear or enhance love?"** That's how you know if something is supporting your emotional, physical, psychological, and spiritual well-being.

The fact that society has created a stigma around God and religion has presented some terrible confusion. The projection that people of faith aren't progressive, inclusive, or tolerant is false and dangerous. After all, every single person is spiritual. Should we try to denounce that part of ourselves, then we lose a communal foundation for love and morality.

When we let society determine personal decisions about who we are and what we believe, then we turn over our health, values, power, peace, freedom, happiness, and independence to a very shallow world. If social acceptance requires us to deny our spirituality, then we will experience a slow, painful breakdown in our personal lives and society. We shall lose the fundamental values that hold us together ... civility, kindness, respect, authenticity, and unconditional love.

The world won't know peace until we recognize that each person has an equal place in this collective. This is where everyone's well-being matters. The only philosophy that supports this type of unconditional love and inclusion is spirituality. Society can label it any way they choose, but when you understand that a power greater than yourself brought you here to share time, energy, and love, it elevates your entire perspective.

Human beings fail to recognize how miraculous that really is, and so it becomes easier to fall into a negative mindset. When people have nothing to lose, they take on the mentality of the survivalist. All decisions are made from a place of fear. We can't have a society filled with survivalists. It's like putting a bone in the middle of a room with a bunch of hungry dogs. People become more consumed with what is "mine" instead of what is in their best interest.

Sadly, the institutions profiting from fear are not invested in your well-being or happiness. They tell divisive stories and make you believe that life is unfair. However, when we settle into a victim mentality, we are essentially giving ourselves permission to sit out, give up, stop working on ourselves, abandon the fight for personal freedoms, quit on relationships, cast aside our responsibilities, and relinquish all hopes, dreams, gifts, and talents.

When people aren't willing to challenge these norms or push through uncomfortable experiences, they never see what it feels like to overcome obstacles, feel liberation, cross a finish line, or experience spiritual redemption. There will be times in your life when you feel like everything is unraveling or falling apart, but those moments are calling you to go deeper. When you stand on your own two feet and realize that you are owed nothing, your role in this world changes dramatically. You stop following the crowd and become a leader, innovator, healer, and unifier.

I think we've postponed our happiness and well-being long enough. The good news is that you have everything you need to make peace with yourself and anything else in the world that needs your love, acceptance, or forgiveness. **We're all carrying**

something heavy and burdensome. Whether that pain represents trauma, separation, addiction, personal mistakes, dysfunctional family systems, old secrets, or new secrets, there is
nothing that you cannot overcome when you are in partnership with God.

Now, that's incredible news for the person who has felt like they
are battling grief or injustice all alone. It may surprise you to learn
that we are breaking down old belief systems that no longer work.
Believe it or not, we are on the verge of a great shift in consciousness. People are waking up to their current surroundings and finding the courage to question these so-called rules that insist on social compliance. In truth, they have made us entitled, codependent, and lazy.

I want to go back to the beginning of this chapter when I talked
about the need to hold on. What I have come to learn is that fear,
survival, and attachments often lead to some physical breakdown
or emotional collapse. The difference between that girl who was
holding onto the golf cart and life so intensely and the person who
stands in her power writing this book … is spirituality.

When I talk about resilience, I am not just referring to your sensibility and fortitude. I am also referring to your inner knowing,
being aware of what you feel, readjusting your expectations to
match the situation in front of you, and allowing your higher
power to be a part of your transformation. This entire human experience is raising your awareness, showing you what matters, and
helping you achieve your greatest potential.

**It's important for you to know what constitutes resilience and
how it actually differs from fear. There are three pieces to resilience:**

1) **Flexibility**: This means that you are not attached to any single outcome, and **you release expectations of how life should be or how others should treat you.** Open-mindedness allows you to see that your hardships are not personal. This allows you to trust that everything unfolds with divine timing and purpose … even the things that are heavy and burdensome.

2) **Acceptance**: This means that you can acknowledge a situation or problem for what it is in its raw state. There is no need for any filters, explanations, or apologies. Allowing a truth to stand on its own is liberating because it frees up your energy from hiding parts of yourself. Once you allow something to be, you can create separation and assess how you actually feel about it. You are essentially creating space for healing or forgiveness. It allows you to release any shame or judgment you have placed on yourself. This is when you can transmute from fear to love.

3) **Purpose:** This means that you are able to step back from what has happened and consult your divine guidance for answers. This is an important stage of resilience because you are choosing to seek wisdom and healing from within. It expands your current perception of life, mortality, imperfection, and the human condition. Each time you experience a deeper level of questioning, you are acquiring wisdom because spiritual answers go well beyond your preconceived ideas of the world.

Just like every other muscle in your body, you can strengthen your resilience. Each time you turn inward to seek comfort and answers from within, you are, in fact, bolstering your self-confidence, elevating your vibration, and developing a closer relationship with God.

It's an interesting time to live in this world. People are equally afraid to live as they are afraid to die. You might say that this conversation is meant to open your eyes to a larger phenomenon being ignored. We are a society that has allowed fear to rule our decisions and well-being.

Despite all these challenges and competing forces that have come into play, there's a strong counter-movement happening. People are realizing that resilience and spirituality are the pathways to inner peace and freedom.

There will always be obstacles to overcome, stress to manage, and losses to grieve. The greatest wisdom that faith has for you is to trust the process and loosen up your tight grip. Fear will always take you backward, and love will always bring you forward. When you understand that truth, everything gets lighter.

And so it is … The next time you feel that urge to hold onto life really tightly, do me a favor,

take a deep breath …

relax your body …

and lean in.

Stay Light.

Love,

Krista

Questions & Reflection

You are invited to pull out your journal and answer the questions below. Write as much as you can before moving on to each new question. Challenge yourself to get in touch with your emotions. What is that truth that needs expression? This is an opportunity to come clean on something that has lingered for way too long.

This process is just for you, so don't hold back. Write down everything that comes into your awareness. Do not worry about editing your feelings. Your higher self brought you to this moment on purpose. Something inside you is ready to crack wide open, and all you have to do is lean in. You might discover that you have multiple things to heal. Feel free to repeat the process as many times as needed.

- **What experience has dramatically changed who you are?**

- **Who or what has made you feel unsafe?**

- **Who or what has made you feel like you aren't good enough?**

- **How can God support you in your healing process?**

- **What do you need from yourself to shift the pain to acceptance and love?**

Chapter Fifteen

"I'm Fine"

So, let's take a quick survey. I want to invite you to read each question below and assess whether you can relate to the experience. Acknowledge each question with a simple **"Yes"** or **"No."** You are welcome to write things down in your journal, or you can just do it in your head.

Here we go ~

- Have you walked through the loss of a family member?

- Have you ever felt helpless in witnessing a loved one suffer through their addiction?

- Have you dealt with the heartbreak of a friendship coming to an abrupt end?

- Have you ever had an experience where you felt deeply disturbed or anxious by what was happening in the world?

- Can you remember a time when you were so emotionally exhausted that you needed to skip a day of school or work?

- **Have you been in a situation where you felt like you were barely holding it together, so much so that you had to fight back your tears?**

I would actually be pretty surprised if you said **"No"** to any of those questions. Every one of those situations represents an uncomfortable experience. There's not a day that goes by that we aren't invited to check in with our feelings, **"How does this make me feel?"** The follow-up question is, **"Am I being invited to stretch myself in some way?"**

This is all a part of our spiritual transformation, where we are invited to become more self-aware and conscious of how we treat ourselves and one another. Unlike any other species, human beings feel so many different emotions, and we can express ourselves. Sometimes, it's verbal (sounds and words). Other times, it's nonverbal (body language and facial expressions). We can express ourselves through music, laughter, and creativity, and on occasion, it may even come out in the form of tears.

I read a quote not too long ago from Scott Kiloby that said, **"Wisdom doesn't come from knowing anything. It comes from feeling everything."** That's a powerful perspective, as it helps you understand that life is circular when it comes to adversity. What feels intensely sad and personal holds some incredible gift to expand your wisdom and consciousness.

Crying is one of the most cathartic things that we can do as human beings. It's a natural part of our healing process. When we experience intense arousal, the limbic system sends a signal to your brain's message center to activate those tiny droplets of water known as emotional tears. Most of us don't realize it, but all those tears we've all been holding back may be the very best mechanism that we have as human beings to self-soothe.

High vibrational emotions can make us cry. We call those **"Tears of Joy."** These tears might fall after you have a tender exchange with your partner, child, parent, sibling, friend, or even a complete stranger who comes to your emotional aid. Happy tears are likely to come when you experience a personal triumph or team victory. You might cry once you've gotten to the other side of a personal hardship or illness.

Some people well up in tears when they profess their love to another person or when they experience something nostalgic, attend a wedding, cross the finish line of a triathlon, or witness a new baby coming into the world. Tears of joy are much easier to express than those associated with sadness, grief, fear, compassion, concern, or physical pain.

So much of our growth, healing, and happiness rely on the permission to have our tears ... all of them. They not only help us stay in touch with high vibrational emotions like love, gratitude, and joy, but they also help us move forward. There are infinite reasons we may deny our tears, starting with the perception of frailty. We have been conditioned to believe that vulnerability is a sign of weakness.

I'm not sure that anyone has ever said this to you before, but everyone needs to hear this: **"Crying is natural. It's the way that your body restores balance (homeostasis). If you can stop holding in your tears, judging yourself, and trying to be strong for everyone else, then you will heal whatever grief you're holding onto. It's a pathway to peace."**

Here are some additional benefits you may not have known about your tears.

- Tears make us feel better by activating our Parasympathetic Nervous Response, which calms us down when we are in a **Fight or Flight Stress Response.**

- Tears detoxify the body by releasing stress hormones and other toxins. We always feel more relaxed after an intense cry.

- Tears allow us to release the pain that we have been holding inside. **"The Feel-Good Hormones"** (endorphins and oxytocin) help dull pain or take it away completely.

- Tears restore balance. They take away the edge associated with stress and the feeling of being overwhelmed.

- Tears improve our mood because they reduce anger, pent-up resentments, fear, and worry. Once there is a release of this energy, the human spirit is immediately lifted.

- Tears have a calming effect, promoting better sleep, immunity, and improved body function.

- Tears create interpersonal benefits. It is an opportunity to bond socially and share experiences and stories with other human beings. The emotional display will often trigger help and support.[15]

That knee-jerk response to choke back your tears to avoid vulnerability, judgment, or embarrassment may be causing you more harm than you know. Tears help you remove stress, release grief and sadness, and help you process trauma. To hold in those tears

---

[15] Anjali Singh, "7 Surprising Benefits of Crying That You Did Not Know," Calm Sage - Your Guide to Mental and Emotional Well-being, November 9, 2021, https://www.calmsage.com/surprising-benefits-of-crying/.

is to reject some part of yourself. It takes away precious reserves of energy from other vital systems in your body, and this makes you the perfect candidate for stress, high blood pressure, insomnia, sickness, and other ailments.

So what happens when you hold back your tears over time? Well, you can become depressed, resentful, or passive-aggressive. You may not stay in one place for too long because you don't want anyone to get too close to hurt you again. The problem with holding everything in is that your emotions become tangled up, and you are likely to become impatient with yourself and other people. This can make you ultra-sensitive, where everyone pushes your buttons and triggers an emotional response.

Now, that's a hot word, **"trigger."** It represents someone or something outside of you that reopens an old wound that hasn't been dealt with. It could be grief, family pain, unresolved trauma, or some heavier emotions that were never settled. If you are somebody who can't seem to go below the surface to meet your feelings, then you'll be triggered all your life, and you're likely to take everything personally.

This is a rough road for those determined to protect their family secrets, stuff their feelings away, or pretend to be fine. However, reality has a way of catching up to us. The Universe may bring a new character to your life to stir up things. You might find yourself in a familiar dynamic that causes you stress and anxiety. It might be your co-worker who rubs you the wrong way or perhaps your neighbor who reminds you of someone who let you down in your life. All of a sudden, you're forced to look at your feelings again … you know, those ones that you buried years before.

It may seem like some terrible twist of fate, and it would be reasonable to stay clear of these people who irritate you. It's just easier to remove them from your life, but guess what? They're not the cause of your inner pain. They are just shining a light on it. You might try to stay clear of anyone who tries to pull back the curtain on your grief or pain, but that doesn't relieve you of your sadness.

We mislabel people all the time or demonize them simply because we're not ready to deal with our sadness. However, what if these people really aren't our adversaries? What if they're assigned to our lives to help us heal? I'm always amazed how trauma or dysfunction repeats itself through other people simply because we're unwilling to meet ourselves and heal the past.

Secrecy is draining. If you are headstrong in hiding your pain, you risk physical depletion and sickness. That old, reliable car (your body) you have been driving and neglecting will eventually break down. The service station you're looking for won't be a quick fix. It will be some decision on your part to get real and confront something uncomfortable in your life that has been stored away.

When grief finally comes to the surface, you are likely to be confronted with some disturbing reality: someone hurt you, someone didn't protect you, someone abused you, something scared you, someone left you, something devastated you, something rattled your foundation, or you made choices that you aren't proud of.

All of this represents emotional work, where you sort through what happened and how you feel about it. It's a time of surrender because you realize you cannot change what has already happened. It is a time for self-compassion, acceptance, and forgiveness.

When tears break the surface, there's ownership of pain, and healing can ensue. Sadly, there are millions of people who battle with their grief, and it is their mission to ensure that nobody upsets the apple cart. As long as we are in denial or resistant to pain, we can tell ourselves, "It didn't happen. It's not mine." However, the moment we own those tears, there's a reality that sets in that we can never go back to who we once were.

So, what do you tell the person who is unable to grieve the loss of a child or a spouse? What do you say to that friend who has gone through a painful divorce? How about the mom or dad who is struggling with empty nesting? What comfort could you possibly offer to the person who has lost their family member or close friend to cancer? What kind of support could you offer to someone who is absolutely exhausted from providing 24-hour care for a parent with Alzheimer's or dementia?

Well, the first round of advice would go something like this, **"It's okay to have your tears because it's your body's natural way to grieve and get back in balance."** We are going to grieve the loss of people that we love. At some point, we are all going to grieve the loss of our identity as it relates to being a parent, a child, a wife, a husband, a friend, etc. We may grieve the loss of pets, the separation of loved ones, or the loss of innocence. We might grieve mistakes, failures, destruction, disaster, devastation, human suffering, or moral decadence.

To be perfectly honest, there isn't a time when we aren't grieving something. It is a part of the human condition, and so we must treat crying as a natural process to gain clarity and spiritual wisdom and push forward. I would go on to say that whatever facade of strength people think they need to uphold is just an expectation of themselves. It's not humanly possible to be perfect or unemotional.

We might initially choke back our tears because we are in shock or disbelief, but when we completely deny or ignore the expression of grief, we just extend our suffering. This affects our well-being. It can cause rumination in our mind, it can affect us physically, causing a variety of health issues, or it can affect us energetically, where our spirit drops and we feel dense.

It's interesting to listen to the way that people characterize themselves around crying. Some people cry at the drop of a hat. They can easily bawl their eyes out, but they fear giving any kind of impression they're soft or weak. It's amazing how many people have some memory or childhood experience in which another person judged or corrected them for crying. Labels like **"Cry Baby, Emotional Wreck, Whiner, or Wimp"** are all derogatory terms that stick over time unless a person has the courage to look inward and dismantle those judgments and characterizations.

Of course, the other extreme is the person who never cries. They don't get off easy. They also get judged. They are seen as unemotional, apathetic, or indifferent. They may be prematurely labeled as **"Cold"** or **"Not Loving."** The problem with these labels is that they're not true, and they just reinforce inadequacy and mismanagement. Needless to say, human beings carry way too much judgment about crying and expressing grief.

Sadly, this dilemma of whether we should cry or not cry presents so much conflict inside our bodies that we have taken ourselves out of the natural process of grieving. The postponement of grief sits and painfully waits for us. Sadly, it is no longer about the labels that other people assign to us. We take on the role of the bully and aggressor by imposing our own self-judgment.

Think about how many times you have subconsciously answered the question, **"Are you okay?"** with **"I'm fine."** I bring this up because many of us have gotten into that habit. We give the quick answer because we want to take the attention off ourselves. Here's what we must remember: there is no amount of hiding, avoidance, or holding back tears that makes the pain actually go away.

It's the things that disturb or disrupt your comfort zone that actually help you expand because you are forced to look inside yourself, connect with your truth, and make brave decisions. The pressure you put on yourself to stay composed and controlled may be destroying you on the inside.

Eventually, all that running from feelings will catch up to you, and there isn't a pill, drink, vacation, or another person that will make you feel better. The remedy will be that moment when you reconcile your life and allow those tears to **"just be."** It's when you let down your walls and come to terms with that "thing" that you have been avoiding. That is when spirituality holds you.

We need to be okay with falling apart, not because we will stay there, but because it will make us stronger, and we will feel connected to our divine guidance.

It makes no difference what it is. It can be something big or something small. If it has some unbearable aspect to it that you feel you must hide who you are, then it is diminishing your light and health. You may think that you're putting on a brave front for your spouse, children, or other people you care about, but if it comes at the expense of your well-being, then you're no longer modeling strength.

And so it is. The next time you feel like tears are forming in the corner of your eyes, I want to invite you to take a deep breath and let them roll down your face without judgment. Let whatever is happening in your life just be. Know that it is another opportunity to bring in Grace and self-compassion.

Whether those tears flow or not, it won't change anything that has already happened. Keeping your tears inside and pretending to be fine doesn't reverse time, history, trauma, pain, or mistakes. It only impedes your healing and interferes with your joy and peace. Imagine the relief you would feel to release that weight from your chest.

It would be one less battle ...

one less burden to carry ...

and one less charade.

Stay Authentic.

Love,

Krista

Questions & Reflection

During this chapter, you were invited to look closer at your belief system around crying and notice how certain influences, like society, create a judgment about men and women who cry. When you realize that there are so many emotional, physical, spiritual, and healing benefits to crying, you can readjust your thought process to bring in more self-love and acceptance. It's time to pull out that journal of yours and ask yourself the following questions:

1) **What has been your belief system around crying?**

2) **Who or what shaped your beliefs about crying?**

3) **Did anything change for you after you read this chapter?**

4) **Has there been some significant event in your life where you felt it wasn't safe to cry? What held you back, and can you give voice to how you felt at that time? Take as much time as you need, and I encourage you to write from the soul with the understanding that you are safe to express your truth and emotions freely. This is just for you.**

The Flight Plan

*I*f it's okay with you, I would love to pull over for a chapter and just catch our breath. We've been discussing life and dissecting emotional habits. This book is not only about your emotional freedom but also about taking some larger responsibility for the vibration in your life. I'm referring to your relationships, your home, your workplace, and the social settings that you influence.

Human beings exchange energy all day long, and it doesn't have to be in person. We feel people's energy via news outlets, media posts, movies, television shows, articles, newspapers, magazines, books, music, etc. We are not only sensitive to sound, tone, and words, but we are also reactive to silence. We absolutely know when something doesn't feel right.

This is why I make the point that humans are multidimensional. Your energy, emotions, experience, knowledge, beliefs, intuition, and spirituality come into play every time you interact with someone. You know what feels genuine or forced … joyful or uncomfortable. You are not only processing things on an intellectual and sensory level, but you are also filtering feelings and experiences through your toolbox.

It's like one big emotional colander. Some things will move through gently, and other things will get stuck and require more assistance. As you become more comfortable with yourself and heal painful experiences from your life, you give others permission to take care of themselves too. It's the theory of a lighthouse. Once you develop wisdom and knowledge, you can guide others in their time of need or darkness. When you recognize this, you understand that your healing extends way beyond your own story.

I first learned about this lighthouse from my mentor, Sunny Dawn Johnston. I never forgot her advice to her students, **"As you heal yourself, you become an example of love and peace for others. You essentially become the lighthouse. You might mirror for others the goodness they do not see in themselves, or you give them a light to follow in their times of darkness."**

I believe it's an honor that we were chosen to live in this particular time and space when we are shifting consciousness in the world. Think about that for a moment. You are here as a result of God's grace and spectacular vision. At various times, you will be asked to be a student. Other times, you will be asked to roll up your sleeves and do work on yourself. Ideally, you will become the one who teaches others about Grace and love. You become a lighthouse.

During this time together, we've broken down certain aspects of life that influence your emotional behaviors. Social conditioning, family systems, generational ties, and the influence of social media and technology play a tremendous part in your habits. We also talked about the unraveling of self, inter-FEAR-ence, and the ongoing choice between survival and spirituality.

Everything is energy, and it's supposed to flow through you. It makes no difference whether you perceive it to be positive or negative. If you hold it, restrict it, or deny it from moving through you, then you are altering the possibilities for love and spiritual expansion. It is empowering to understand this truth because your free will comes into play every single day. You get to choose love and good energy for yourself.

There aren't enough people who identify themselves with love. In reality, if self-love and emotional healing were a greater priority in today's world, we would have fewer conflicts, sickness, mental health problems, separation, stress, domestic violence, addictions, and social unrest.

I loved sharing my mother-in-law's story about **"Spiritual Redemption."** Peace cannot exist until we learn to surrender what we cannot control in our lives. Catherine's graceful release of this life taught us to trust our faith and see beyond the physical world. Her story reminds us to silence the ego that wants to be in charge, control storms, and superintend others.

We learned that the way people treat us has little to do with us. It is a reflection of their own emotional capacity. People can only meet us as far as they are willing to meet themselves, and we cannot push anyone into their healing. They must want it for themselves. It makes no difference how much we love them.

In general, it is just a good practice to release our attachments to how we think life or other people should be. **"Shoulds"** can get us into trouble because once we tell our brain that there's only one possible outcome, we get disappointed when it doesn't happen that way. Allowing the Universe to play some larger part in your experience is freeing. Not only does it take away the pressure to be perfect, but it opens the door to other magical possibilities.

During our time together, we also took a look inside those old emotional toolboxes. We decided that some of the judgments, rules, and habits that we are still carrying around with us are no longer serving our current needs. Self-inquiry is critical to understanding what is useful to your life and what is no longer working.

The goal is to expand consciousness and become more resilient, but this won't happen without reflection and reconciliation of your energy coming and going.

From there, we talked about emotional knots and how to untangle energy and process difficult emotions like sadness, anxiety, grief, and frustration. Any fear trapped in your psyche or body will hold you back somewhere in your life. This is why it's important to allow those tears to fall when they come up. They keep you grounded in reality, and they allow you to heal difficult aspects of your life.

Nobody else can decide what it means to be the best version of yourself. It's a private journey that you take with your higher power. As much as we would all like to hold onto old parts of our lives, we can't. That's a hard one for many people who are grieving changes in their story, or are missing their loved ones that have gone to the other side.

This life you have come to know, rely upon, and grow deeply attached to will eventually change ... and so will the people around you. However challenging things get, you must remember how resilient you are and how powerful faith is. For those who have a difficult time letting go, here's an analogy that may be helpful.

"The Flight Plan"

Your flight plan is already arranged. You may not have full control over all your stops or the passengers seated around you, but you will participate heavily in this experience. You see, there are no direct flights to Heaven. You will need to change planes several times throughout your journey. Some layovers will be quick and easy. Others will be long and taxing. Some people you love might even get off the plane before you do. See their departure as a graduation.

Each time you move through change or adversity, you will need to reorganize your luggage. You'll need to make some hard decisions ... what you want to bring with you ... and what you would like to release. Some of those things will relate to your identity, or they might represent relationships that have come to an end. It's all okay. Eventually, all physical things will be left behind, and all emotional burdens will be turned over to the pilot (God).

In that final leg of your journey, there will be just one part of yourself left. It will be your soul. At that pinnacle moment, you will not have any time left to undo, repair, or revise your experience, and you won't be able to go back and do all those things that you postponed. Your goal is to be at peace with every place you've been and leave nothing unsaid or unfinished, particularly with the people you love.

So, here's some quick traveling advice. Pack light and stay aligned with your heart because it will direct you to people and causes that are meaningful to your life. Listen to your inner guidance. When something doesn't feel in alignment, speak up. Do not make assumptions about other people ... who they are, or what they feel. Instead, ask them what they need to make their flight more comfortable. Be very clear and decisive about what you need to feel safe and secure.

Expect turbulence. Take slow, deep breaths to calm your nervous system down. Trust that the pilot has your best interest. Everything will eventually stabilize, and you'll arrive exactly where you need to go next. Time is measured on earth, but it doesn't exist in the next realm. I guarantee that there are never enough hours in the day to do everything you want, so you must choose to use your energy wisely.

Invest in people and situations that share your values and support you to become a better person. Don't wait until the very end of your life to make peace with yourself, other people, or God, for you never know when your plane will make its final descent. Live what you love right now.

In the end, you have a complete say in whether you choose to be in alignment with your soul's journey or you accumulate more physical and emotional baggage. If you can hold space for God and stay open to love at all times, you will expand in the most glorious ways. You will see the most spectacular places and experience the most extraordinary things. Trust that there are no accidents and that this flight was specifically assigned to you.

Once you have arrived at that place of inner knowing, you will see that you have had a tremendous impact on everyone around you. For now, take your seat and buckle up. The caution lights will turn off shortly, and you will be able to move around the cabin freely.

Enjoy your flight.

If you're starting to see a new picture of yourself and the world, that's wonderful. If I'm being honest, writing this book has surprised me. What began as a journey to help myself and others learn how to manage stress and heal wounds from the past has turned out to be a book about God. The more I wrote about him, the more clarity I found about the meaning of life.

Somehow, **The Search for Grace** opened something inside of me that is gentle, forgiving, and miraculous. This experience has helped me understand what was lacking in myself and what is currently lacking in the world, and that is LOVE. There aren't enough places where we can have conversations like these. As you can see, spirituality is vital to your health, happiness, and legacy.

If I were to ask you what is most important to you … love or fear, you would easily choose **"LOVE."** Everybody would choose love, and yet, time and time again, we choose fear, chaos, resentment, anger, and other low vibrational energies. It's not that we don't know any better. We often resort to what is familiar and encoded in our memories and psyche.

With each new day, you get to wake up and choose love. If you find yourself stressed all the time and do not feel supported, you have an amazing opportunity to reprogram your thoughts, beliefs, and attitude. If you can start clearing some of that dense energy you are carrying and releasing some of that emotional luggage you have been collecting, you will find yourself much better off. You'll have more time for your joys, lists, and the relationships that raise your vibration.

The Universe is ready to support and hold you. It's just a matter of consciously allowing space in your heart for it to work its magic. You are at a crossroad, my friend, and you get to decide how this entire flight experience goes. Just remember that you have the very best pilot available.

Stay Glorious.

Love,

Krista

Personal Reflection/Drawing Exercise 16

This next exercise requires three blank sheets of white paper, a simple box of crayons, your phone to set the timer, a pen, and your journal.

This is a four-part exercise. As we stated earlier, let go of any judgment that you might have about your drawing skills. This is a free-flowing exercise. The greater purpose of this activity is to allow color and images to fill the page and tap into your inner guidance. This is an exercise that you simply cannot do wrong.

Part 1: Put a small #1 in the upper right-hand corner on one of the blank sheets of paper. Now, set your timer for six minutes. Use your crayons to draw how you see yourself today. You may interpret this exercise any way you want. Hit start on your timer and color until the six minutes are up. Stop drawing or coloring when the timer ends, even if the picture doesn't feel finished. Then, turn your paper over and set it aside for the second part of this exercise.

Part 2: Put a small #2 in the upper right-hand corner of another blank sheet of paper. Now, set your timer for six minutes. Use your crayons to draw yourself with your greatest problem. You may interpret this exercise in any way that you want. Hit start on your timer and color until the six minutes are up. Stop drawing or coloring when the timer ends, even if the picture doesn't feel quite finished.

Part 3: Put a small #3 in the upper right-hand corner of the final blank sheet of paper. Now, set your timer for six minutes. Use

---

[16] This drawing exercise was adapted from my Mind-Body Medicine training. Some of the verbiage has been modified to reinforce the content of this chapter.

your crayons to draw yourself with your problem solved. Hit start on your timer and color until the six minutes are up. You will need to stop drawing or coloring when the timer ends, even if the picture doesn't feel quite finished.

Part 4: Lay out all three pictures in front of you and allow all messages to come through. Study each picture for several minutes and notice how you feel. Are there any observations you have about your drawings? Did you learn something new? This is the time that you want to pull out your journal and document any thoughts, feelings, and interpretations you have. Remember that there are no right or wrong answers.

Is there some new clarity about the problem that you have been carrying around with you?

Has there been an energetic shift of any kind as a result of this drawing exercise?

Did your inner guidance come through and offer some valuable support or advice?

How do you now feel about the problem that was troubling your heart?

Chapter Seventeen

The Unsung Hero

To say that we are juggling a lot is an understatement. We typically have about five to six balls in the air at all times. Whether it's family commitments, work obligations, financial responsibilities, home maintenance, or social gatherings, our calendars are pretty full, which often means our minds are racing too.

Recently, I've been reflecting on who **"The Unsung Hero"** is in all of our stories. What's holding all of this together? How are we able to keep going physically and emotionally? Well, the answer may surprise you. It's none other than the human body. That's probably not the answer you were thinking about, but here we are in a world that demands everything of us, and somehow, these bodies of ours keep showing up.

The human body is nothing short of miraculous. You would think that for all the intense work it's doing to keep us in balance, we would be completely dialed into self-care and appreciation. Sadly, it's quite the opposite. Most of us aren't very attentive to our body's needs. We rarely thank our bodies, pamper them, or show proper gratitude for all that it does to support our activities and lifestyle.

So why do we pay so little attention? The short answer is that we get so caught up in keeping those balls in the air, we tend to over-look the role our body has in our health, happiness, and stabiliza-tion. Most of us don't view ourselves in a relationship with our body. You might say that things have become a bit one-sided. Our bodies are working tirelessly to keep up, and most of the time, we are oblivious to what it needs.

Like any relationship, there has to be more give and take if we are going to grow old together.

Without a healthy body, we simply won't have the same pleasures, options, or conveniences. Most of us take it for granted that our body will just keep doing its job with very little supervision or maintenance.

It's because of the body that we have the luxury to move, laugh and sing. The body helps us nourish ourselves physically, intellec-tually, and spiritually. It enables us to experience a full range of emotions and engage with people, animals, and nature. It's be-cause of our bodies that we're able to use our five different senses and tap into our clairvoyant senses (intuition and psychic abili-ties).

That body of yours isn't just a pretty shell ... it protects you from threats, extreme elements, illness, and unsafe conditions. It also facilitates connection, enables you to experience intimacy and sex-ual pleasure, and, best of all, it has the wisdom to self-heal.

Despite our busy schedules and all the crazy demands, it shows up every single day. It's ready to go to battle for us, and somehow, it always knows what to do. It operates with very little assistance. We don't have to remind ourselves to pump blood, digest, or breathe. The body just handles it. So much of what the body does is automatic, yet it is highly influenced by our thoughts, emo-tions, and energy.

Whatever you tell the body to focus on becomes its primary interest. You can tell it to focus on joy or sadness, fear or love, good health or sickness. It's entirely up to you. One could use the analogy of sitting in a director's chair. In every situation, we are directing our body at all times, and it coordinates around our mood, environment, and energy.

If you complain that you're exhausted, your body reinforces that condition. You're likely to feel depleted and heavy by the end of the day. If you say out loud that you're pissed off, sick, stuck, overwhelmed, afraid, fat, or stressed out, your body will affirm those experiences too. Words are powerful, and your physical condition is greatly influenced by fear, self-criticism, stress, and pressure.

It's much more productive for us to affirm how we want to feel. **"Today, I feel strong, joyful, calm, well-rested, and at ease."** So, what do you do if you're having a bad day or physically struggling? That's when you can give your body something to strive for. **"I'm attracting positive experiences to me that are healthy, peaceful, energizing and fulfilling."** Treating your body like a friend is incredibly impactful. Every time you administer self-compassion or kindness to yourself, you are elevating your vibration and immunity.

Here's the reality: if you don't pay attention to your energy, inner dialogue, or what you are absorbing from the rest of the world then your body will make interpretations for you. How many times have you caught yourself saying something along these lines?

"I'm overwhelmed!"

"I feel like crap today!"

"I'm soooo stressed out!"

You may think you're just blowing off a little steam, but if that is the only messaging you give your body all day long, then you are affirming sickness, stress, and density in your body. Many people don't even realize how they are directing their overall experience in their bodies or how they might be attracting chaos and drama to themselves.

Make no mistake about it: the human body is not only listening to everything you say, but it's also communicating new information all the time. If I had to pinpoint the lapse in communication, I would say that we don't sit still long enough to listen to what it wants us to know. If we are ignoring our bodies, then we can also assume that we are tuning out God as well.

Listening to your divine guidance is so important to your health and well-being. It not only gives you advice on what is in your best interest, but it will advise you on what to release from your worry. If you abandon your spirituality, you are essentially severing ties to that part of you that finds deeper meaning for adversity or loss.

It may be a strong declaration on my part, but this lack of inner listening and spirituality explains why our world has become so sick, compromised, and desensitized. If we can't recognize our pain and sadness, then how can we possibly be compassionate or empathetic to others? How can we possibly find solutions for societal problems when so many people are avoiding their own inner conflict?

We have essentially made pain and stress full-time guests in our bodies. Many of us have been carrying around our pain for so long that we have no recall of what it feels like to be light or free. When we let pain stay for too long, it affects our self-esteem and our entire mindset. It makes us believe we aren't worthy of good health, love, or abundance. We become lethargic about life.

So, what are some things that your body might be trying to tell you right now? I've compiled a list of common complaints that reflect physical discomfort, some basic needs relating to hydration, nourishment, rest, or an emotional need. As you go through this list, ask yourself if any of these sound familiar. At some point, you may have dismissed a similar message from your body.

"I need some water."

"I'm so tired!"

"I'm scared right now!"

"I can't breathe!"

"I'm uncomfortable. I think we need to go home."

"These pants are way too tight."

"Could you please stop trying to please everyone? It's exhausting."

"I'm worried about something, and my stomach hurts."

"I have a terrible feeling about that guy. Keep your space and your guard up."

"My back is killing me. You're going to need some support!"

"I can't sleep. I have too much on my mind."

"I need you to slow down."

"My joints are stiff. I could really use a walk in nature."

"Just so you know, I cannot keep up with everyone else!"

"I need to release these feelings now!"

"Go ahead. Add one more thing to my plate, and I'm going to explode!"

Now, whether or not you believe that your body speaks to you in this manner is neither here nor there. The larger takeaway is that your body is very expressive, and it communicates with you all the time. I want to invite you to think about what it would be like to sit down at the kitchen table and have a conversation with your body. What would it say to you about the way that you have been caring for it, and what does it need from you at this particular time?

We might attribute disconnection to the hectic pace we keep, but it may go much deeper. If you're somebody who can't sit still, you carry a lot of fear, stress, or worry, or you tend to hold in your emotions, then you are likely to miss incoming messages. Here's another thought: you may have gotten used to ignoring messages from your body because you're unwilling to address that grief that you have stored away.

The body will nudge you when something is out of alignment. It's when you ignore these signs or early symptoms that serious health issues can arise. There is an emotional connection to everything happening in your body, particularly when you are stressed out, afraid, heartbroken, conflicted, grief-stricken, or worried. The moment you experience these heavier emotions, you become vulnerable to sickness, physical ailments, and disease.

Now, the word **"disease"** has a dual meaning. It can refer to an illness or disorder, but it also means that something is out of alignment. There is a serious **"DIS-EASE"** in the body. Something needs to be acknowledged, healed, and released in order for you to feel healthy and harmonious again.

One of my favorite books is called *The Secret Language of Your Body.* The author of the book, Inna Segal, talks about the relationship between emotions and physical manifestations. Whether it's physical pain, depression, exhaustion, disease, autoimmune issues, weight issues, inflammation, rashes, migraines, or sleep disorders, every symptom can give you feedback about where your emotions are.

Of course, there are infinite scenarios in which physical pain or ailments can be traced back to unexpressed emotions. Earlier in the book, I shared something pretty vulnerable. I developed asthma as a teen. I now understand that it was a physical embodiment of fear. Holding my breath was a survival behavior that I took on when I felt upset or scared, and that distress manifested into spasms in the bronchi of my lungs. I told myself that I couldn't breathe, so my body registered that message and carried out my direction to the fullest.

What I now know for sure is that we cannot suppress pain, fear, or emotions in our bodies indefinitely. It's just not sustainable. The body can only keep the lid closed for so long. It needs to get back into balance (homeostasis). It will literally get our attention by sidelining us with a physical problem, ailment, or diagnosis.

If the body gets sick, it's because all previous warning signs have been ignored. It's begging us to pull over and pay attention to our emotions. In other words, we've got to take care of our shit! Now, that might be something trivial like catching up on laundry, changing a broken tail light, or cleaning your refrigerator, but it could also be something more pressing like mending a family conflict, confronting an addiction, finding a new job, or dealing with the grief of a close friend who's passed away.

As far as the body is concerned, it's all nonpersonal. It just knows that something is interfering with homeostasis. It's fascinating how we can ignore something uncomfortable or traumatic for years, but not the body. It will eventually resort to tough love and get our attention with a symptom or ailment. It's basically alerting us to stop everything and pay attention to our emotions because it's done placating us. **"You cannot ignore this any longer. You need to take care of this right now!"**

If you're somebody who has been stockpiling emotions and traumas your whole life, your body might start screaming for attention by manifesting a disease, disorder, physical ailment, or autoimmune issue. If you're someone who worries all the time, your body might get your attention with headaches or migraines, or if you're somebody who has trouble confronting people or saying "No," then your body might get your attention with symptoms that affect your throat. You might be prone to coughs, laryngitis, or sore throats.

The symptoms are always real, but behind the actual sickness, there may be something burning inside. It could represent unexpressed anger, hurt feelings, fear, repressed trauma, or guilt. The interesting point is that the body won't play along for too long. It will eventually break its silence.

Most of us have adopted a Western approach to medicine where we treat the symptoms with a pill, so we often miss the real reason that we become vulnerable to sickness. There's simply no telling how your body will respond to traumas or grief, but the tighter you hold onto your pain, the more susceptible you become to exhaustion, hypersensitivity, inflammation, spasms, disease, and aching in the body.

Inner conflict sabotages people all the time because they have stopped being true to themselves. When you mask your pain, you are likely to blame your health problems on terrible circum-

stances, shitty misfortune, a busy schedule, genetics, or other people. This takes you off the hook for any emotional accountability.

Inna Segal talks about various emotional conditions and refers to
the body's innate wisdom to heal itself. However, healing is pred-
icated on a person's willingness to pay attention to their body, be
observant of warning signs, and take ownership of their emotions.
There are a number of questions that you can ask yourself to gain
insight into your own body's needs.

JOURNAL QUESTIONS:

*I encourage you to read these questions to yourself and then
answer them in your journal. Feel free to write as much as you
need to satisfy each question for yourself.*

- "Do I need rest, hydration, or support?" If so, elaborate
  on how you can resolve this for yourself.

- "Do I need to come to terms with anything upsetting?"

- "Are there any tears that I have been holding in?"

- "What are the feelings that I have pushed down that are
  now ready to be released?"

- "Is there a feeling of loss or disappointment that needs to
  be acknowledged?"

- "Am I harboring anger or resentment?"

- "Do I need to grieve a relationship that ended abruptly?"

- "Is there someone in my life that I need to stand up to?"

- "Do I need to own a mistake or failure?"

- "Do I need to release guilt or shame?"

- "Do I need to offer forgiveness to myself or another person?"

- "Is there something in my life that needs closure?"

Because your body is in sync with your higher power, it already knows what you need to heal. When you invoke this wisdom, you will receive the guidance necessary for your inner peace.

We are the ones who create safety inside our body. We do this through self-love and spirituality. That's where we find the courage to pull off that lid that has been holding onto grief, painful memories, and secrets. And while it may seem senseless to rehash the past or open Pandora's Box, I promise you that it will set you free, not because it completely removes pain from your story, but because once and for all, you will be able to stand in your truth.

Your life experiences are just taking you further along in your transformation, and it is by the grace of God that you gain wisdom from those hardships. Everything happens with some greater purpose, even if you don't understand it at the moment when your life is unraveling. The reason that our bodies are working so hard most of the time is because we are expending so much energy in trying to hide our emotions and circumvent grief.

The problem with this scenario is that we are not just resisting pain, we are also resisting a critical part of ourselves that is spiritual and connected to God. Whether you are digging yourself out of a financial hole, starting over after ending a relationship, finding a job, confronting addiction, losing weight, sorting through family drama, struggling to get back on your feet again, restoring your health, coming to terms with grief, or making peace with old traumas in your life, it's all yours, and you can't run.

It will require every bit of your courage to address wounds, but once you surrender that situation over to God then your body can start the recovery process. When you stop hiding your truth or apologizing for who you are or what you feel, you can begin to put things in place that actually support your body, mental health, and spiritual well-being. Without that honesty, you can't be real.

It's just not enough to say, "I'm stressed out." That feeling of being tired and overwhelmed is always a symptom of something else going on in your life. You can't feel better until you acknowledge what is upsetting you on a deeper level.

I'm going to go out on a limb and share one more personal example of a condition that was born out of fear. When I was in my late thirties, I was raising my sons, running a sandwich shop with my husband, and serving as the president of a local nonprofit called "The Fabulous Women of Sonoma County." I loved being a mother, business owner, and philanthropist. However, any one of those things on their own would have been a lot to manage. Well, I was overambitious and ran all three at the same time.

To say that I put way too much pressure on myself is an understatement. I took on way too much at one time, and yet I still expected the highest performance from myself. I had trouble asking for help. My expectations and perfectionism left me exhausted all the time. I hate to say it, but I grew resentful. With that frustration came these unusual rashes all over my hands and fingers. The itching was unbearable, and many times, my fingers would crack and bleed.

Now, if I'm being completely honest, I was embarrassed by this condition, so I hid it from most people. It became my big little secret. It really wasn't until I started studying the connection between the mind, body, and spirit that I found the clarity I needed to understand this mystery skin condition. My early assessment was that I had shitty genes, and I chalked it up to an allergy. If anybody asked about it, I would tell them that I was allergic to the latex gloves at my work.

While I may have had some precondition to allergies, the reason for the rashes was much deeper. I did an exercise in which I was invited to draw out a picture of what stress felt like in my body. Of course, I drew my hands with ugly bumps and rashes. I used my red crayon to demonstrate how inflamed my hands were. From there, I was able to name my problem and then physically dialogue with my symptoms in a journal.

That exercise was powerful. It offered some deeper revelations about my life. You see, my body was informing me that I was stressed out and deeply irritated. I was in conflict with myself all the time because I couldn't meet all the demands and expectations I imposed on my life. From afar it seemed that I was on top of my game, but upon a closer look, I could see that I was collapsing under the pressure.

Because I had trouble asking for help, I chose to do most things on my own. This made me feel tired, impatient, and frustrated. I was a victim and a martyr, and suddenly, my joy of carpooling, running a household, and running a business and a nonprofit became chores. It wasn't easy, but I finally took the lid off and confronted myself. I came to grips with my truth, my feelings, and my expectations. I was so irritated with myself for taking things that were joyful in my life and turning them into obligations.

It's pretty interesting to reflect on that situation now and see how I was creating drama, resentment, and painful rashes. Believe me, the Universe sent me plenty of signs ahead of time that my body was not happy, but I dismissed every message that suggested that I was over my head or out of control. Eventually, my hands got so bad it hurt to wash them. That was when I could no longer ignore myself.

Once I found out that I was causing my skin condition, I made adjustments to my life and my calendar. I had to learn to let go of certain things, temper my expectations of myself, set aside my ego, and ask for help. I had to forgive myself for taking on way too much. As difficult as it was, I eventually released my nonprofit, my business, and the expectation of perfectionism. And guess what? Those rashes went away.

Imagine how my body felt with all those rules and demands. It was livid, and my skin was proof of the madness. What I didn't realize is that I put myself in direct opposition to my well-being. I essentially became my own worst enemy. So, there's an example from my life where rashes manifested as a result of inner conflict. When I told you in chapter one that I would be doing the work right alongside you, I meant it.

My hope is that this chapter sheds light on your magnificent body and how hard it's working for you. Perhaps you have a new appreciation for your body and all the things it's doing to keep you aligned. I also hope it gives you a new perspective on the relationship between emotional pain and physical illness.

There are infinite ways in which stress can rear itself in the body. The most important action you can take right now is to make an evaluation of your own health. Where do you carry your stress in your body? What symptoms (if any) need your attention and love at this very moment?

In just a moment, I will be taking you through a similar exercise that helped me uncover my own health issues. Before I do so, I want to provide a list of common ailments that we are all likely to experience. Notice which emotions or survival behaviors tend to be linked to these conditions.

Stomach Issues/Possible Contributing Factors: Difficulty digesting life and assimilating new information. Feeling like you got socked in the gut. Feeling stuck, worried, fearful, or guilty. Difficulty expressing yourself, so there are feelings of despair and hopelessness.

Headaches/Possible Contributing Factors: Feeling angry, resistant, frustrated, judgmental, self-critical, or stubborn. Stuck in a limited way of thinking. Unwilling to change. Feeling overburdened with work, responsibilities, and worries. Overwhelmed much of the time. Lots of blocked energy. The need to be right or perfect is exhausting. May feel responsible for everyone else's happiness.

Backaches/Possible Contributing Factors: Feeling unsupported by life and the people around you. Overwhelmed by so much pressure. Very sensitive to other people's judgments and criticisms. Too focused on limitations and survival. Consumed about what is wrong with life instead of what is positive. Worried or insecure about supporting oneself financially. May have unresolved emotions from the past or childhood. This presents difficulty in forgiving oneself and others.

Itching or Rashes/Possible Contributing Factors: Unhappy with what you are doing or where you are in life. Feeling oversensitive, insecure, annoyed, or fearful. Perfectionism, self-imposed limitations, and strict expectations are causing irritation. May have suppressed emotions that can no longer be pushed down.

Sore Throat/Possible Contributing Factors: Feeling unsafe, unworthy, and insecure. Find it difficult to express true feelings.

There is a constant feeling of inner conflict. This contributes to feelings of frustration, fear, resentment, and hopelessness. Something that needed expression was buried away because you had some fear that you wouldn't be supported.

Anxiety Attacks/Possible Contributing Factors: Difficulty in trusting the flow of life. Constantly thinking of the past or future. Feeling insecure, unsupported, and helpless to change the current situation. Focused on fear and limitations.

Constipation/Possible Contributing Factors: Feeling closed off or stuck in some old way of thinking. Tends to hold back and often refuses to change. Resistant to other people's views or opinions. Strong convictions which may be seen as selfish, childish, or demanding. Often feels underappreciated and unloved. Tends to worry about the future.

Shortness of Breath/Possible Contributing Factors: Feeling afraid, anxious, stuck, or disempowered. Absorbent and often controlled by others. Always trying to please other people. Committed to being perfect. Pushing yourself so hard that you are often exhausted and out of breath. Difficulty expressing hurt feelings.

Insomnia/Possible Contributing Factors: Unable to relax your mind and body. Feeling unsafe. Has difficulty letting go. Constantly worrying and ruminating. Often feels scattered and fearful. Harboring guilt and resentment.

Inflammation/Possible Contributing Factors: Experiencing inner conflict and aggravation. Feeling anger and frustration about unconscionable behavior or an injustice you have witnessed.

Seething over something.[17]

Just because your body gets sick doesn't mean that you need a pill or prescription to feel better. Your body may just be calling for your attention, rest, or love, or it might be requesting that you take care of some shit in your life that you have put on hold or neglected.

Know that you have choices in how you care for your physical well-being. The next time you feel a headache, an upset stomach, a sore throat, or discomfort in your body, don't immediately grab the bottle of Advil. Instead, I encourage you to pull out your journal and ask yourself if there is something that you need to heal emotionally. This provides a new discipline for yourself, where you honor your body and take back your power.

Stay Aware.

Love,

Krista

---

[17] Inna Segal, "The Secret Language of Your Body," Atria Books (August 2010), pgs. 19, 51, 101, 126, 148, 149, 159

Personal Reflection/Drawing Exercise[18]

This next exercise requires one sheet of white paper, a simple box of crayons, your phone to set the timer, a pen, and your journal.

PART 1: SOFT BELLY BREATHING

Okay, let's get your supplies ready for another drawing exercise. By now, I think you know what I'm going to say. Be kind to yourself. There is no right or wrong way to do this exercise. Since this drawing relates to your body, it will benefit you to take a few cleansing breaths before you get started. Remember that Soft Belly Breathing is gentle and effortless.

Take in air through the nose slowly and then exhale through your lips. Allow any sounds to happen without judgment. Notice how the air moves through your nose and then fills your lungs with oxygen. You will observe your belly rise during the inhalation and fall during the exhalation. Do this as many times as you need to establish a connection with your body.

PART 2: DRAWING EXERCISE

Set your timer for six minutes. I want to invite you to draw yourself. In this particular exercise, you will answer the following question, **"Where do you carry stress or pain in your body?"** You may interpret this exercise any way you want. You might draw your full body or zero in on a particular area that is vulnerable. Hit start on your timer and color until the six minutes are up. Stop drawing or coloring when the timer ends, even if the picture doesn't feel finished.

---

[18] This drawing exercise was adapted from my Mind-Body Medicine training. Some of the verbiage has been modified to reinforce the content of this chapter.

Upon finishing this exercise, take a few minutes to evaluate your drawing. **Is there a problem, symptom, or issue that revealed itself during this exercise? Does it have a name?**

PART 3: DIALOGUE WITH A SYMPTOM

Once you have a name for your problem, symptom, or ailment (ie: rash, migraine, insomnia, stomach ache, etc.) take a blank journal page and address the page like you are writing a letter to yourself.

Dear [place your first name here]**,**

I am "[place the name of your symptom here]"

and this is what I want you to know ...

I encourage you to approach this exercise with an open mind. It will allow you to tap into your subconscious. As you take the lid off something painful stored in your body, you are likely to receive messages from your inner guidance. You may be advised on what you need to do to get stronger physically, mentally, emotionally, and spiritually. This information will be vital to moving forward, processing grief, finding closure, or releasing something traumatic.

The conversation that happens on paper will often peel back layers of pain that you may have either forgotten about or pushed down a long time ago. You might discover a memory from your childhood or get in touch with a difficult event in your life. Whatever comes up, write it down. Also, do not be worried about grammar or editing your sentences. Just FREE write!

At any point that you would like to ask your symptom a question, feel free to do so. (If it's easier to see, you may alternate pen colors.) Once you have had a full dialogue, thank your problem, symptom, or ailment for helping you better understand yourself. Then, take time to read the conversation and digest the information. This could be a very big turning point in your health.

Chapter Eighteen

"I'm Sorry"

*I*t was a few years ago that we bought our home in Arizona. I loved how the house made me feel. Subconsciously, I knew that it would be the place where my husband and I would retire. I imagined grandkids playing in the yard and swimming in the pool. It was strange how comfortable that house made me feel. I almost felt like I had been there before.

From the day we got the keys from the realtor, I talked about our beautiful tree that was in the yard. Well, it wasn't exactly **"our tree."** It belonged to the neighbor, but it was so massive that it filled our yard with colorful blooms and shade. There was just something about that tree that gave me joy and love.

I can remember that I had all kinds of feelings when I moved out of state. On one hand, it was exciting because we would be closer to our son, Frank, who lived in Arizona. On the other hand, I felt a tremendous sense of loss being further away from my siblings and mother. It may seem strange to say this, but that tree gave me so much comfort. I felt grounded and protected when I was with it. I was going through so much change in my life, but the tree made everything better. It reminded me that everything has a season.

The tree had bright yellow flowers, my dad's favorite color. In some beautiful way, that tree made me feel closer to him and to

God. I really didn't understand it, but I was attached to that tree. I loved how the branches draped over the fence and humming-birds danced around it.

Well, about a year later something startling woke me from my sleep. I can remember hearing the sound of chainsaws. I immediately jumped out of bed. I saw one guy on a ladder and another man at the base of the tree catching falling limbs. I said to my husband, "Oh my God, they're cutting down my tree!"

Paul quickly comforted me, "They're probably just cutting it back." I watched them all day. One by one, branches fell to the ground, and I balled my eyes out. I cried like it was a family member. Grief poured out of me. I told Paul, "I can't believe they would tear down my tree." Respectfully, Paul said, "Honey, it's not your tree. It's their tree." It really didn't register. It didn't matter whose tree it was. It felt like it was a part of me.

A few hours passed, and I got a knock on my front door. It was my neighbor. She wanted to tell me that a falling branch broke one of the cinder blocks on our fence. I stood there motionless with a blank stare. I had tears rolling down my face. She asked me if I was okay. I told her that I wasn't okay and that I loved that tree. She was speechless. I waited for her to say "I'm sorry," but it never came. She told me that the fence would be repaired, and then she left.

The story doesn't actually end there because I was left with a ton of emotions to deal with. I was not only attached to the tree but I was attached to the idea that my neighbor owed me an apology. It took a few weeks, but I eventually came to terms with the truth. I realized that I wasn't actually mad at her. I was just clinging to the anger to avoid my true feelings ... loss and sadness. I was still grieving the death of my father and a life that I once loved.

It's all very interesting how emotional behaviors play a part in self-protection, but they can also delay the grieving process. I was convinced that I deserved an apology from my neighbor, but what I really needed was time to feel my emotions, and I needed to forgive myself. I was holding onto more pain and guilt than I was willing to admit, and none of it had anything to do with her.

The truth is, as I packed up the moving truck in Petaluma, I also packed up all my emotions too. I secretly put them away where nobody would find them. I felt like I had let everyone down by leaving and breaking some sort of family code. I suppose those feelings would have eventually surfaced, but the release of the tree opened a vault of sad feelings. In the end, that beautiful tree gave me everything—a place to rest my weary heart and a powerful lesson in letting go.

It's amazing how we can insulate ourselves from pain and uncomfortable emotions like sadness, guilt, grief, and shame. Subconsciously, we might convince ourselves that we have to be strong for others, or if we stuff down those feelings long enough, then whatever intense sorrow we feel will eventually fade away, but that's not how pain works.

It's certainly not uncommon for us to take on anger when something upsetting has happened. We may reframe traumatic experiences so that we can bear the turmoil or grief. We may tell ourselves that we've been unfairly treated or victimized just so we can get out of bed in the morning. In some cases, we might also take out our anger on God. After all, how could a loving God inflict such horrible pain? Rather than go through some healing process to discover more, some people would rather take on the anger and call it a day.

We may think it's easier to substitute ANGER for grief, loss of innocence, guilt, shame, abuse, abandonment, feeling unsafe, or the disappointment that a loved one didn't show up for us or protect us. When we commit to the story that something unfair has happened to us, we don't have to do any inner work. We can make the entire experience about injustice and blame our heartache on someone else or God.

Anger is just a temporary deflection. Eventually, all those unexpressed tears will need to be dealt with. Otherwise, they'll show up later out of the blue, kinda like the day the tree came down.

Emotions like anger, guilt, resentment, and sadness can pile up and reinforce sickness or physical ailments. It could be the reason for an otherwise healthy person to come down with a very serious diagnosis.

So, here's something to consider. What if the forgiveness that you're waiting for has nothing to do with anybody else? What if you need to forgive yourself? This is typical for the perfectionist or the person who lives in denial. It's difficult for them to own their feelings or mistakes. They have trouble acknowledging frailty, and they can't come to terms when something has run its natural course.

When people can't admit that they've done something wrong, they build up feelings of shame, disappointment, and unworthiness. They subconsciously find ways to punish or sabotage themselves because they don't feel like they are deserving. As you can see, "I'm sorry" is tricky whether you're waiting to receive an apology or you need to give one. When we make self-love and happiness conditional, we place ourselves in an impossible position to be happy or healthy.

It's true; our world would certainly be a better place if more people had the courage to apologize for their mistakes because that means that they're taking ownership of their choices. Given the fact that we have a limited amount of control over what other people do or say, our healing has to stand alone. We need to spend our moments concentrating on what we are doing as opposed to what others aren't doing. We need to study ourselves instead of waiting for others to reconcile with us, and we need to address our feelings for what they really are.

There is nothing that you cannot peacefully resolve within yourself. However, you will not be able to go back to who you once were, and that's probably the toughest part for people to accept. You may want your old life back, but the Universe has redirected you. It may be for some larger purpose that hasn't revealed itself yet. However painful and uncomfortable it all is, it will provide you with an opportunity to expand your consciousness.

So, how do you begin the healing process? Well, you start with an intention. You inform your higher power that you are ready to let go and learn something new about yourself. When you have been holding something in for a long time, you'll need to cut yourself some slack. That means that you invite self-compassion and patience into your heart. That's the gentle piece that is missing, and only you can give it to yourself. Then, you breathe into your vulnerability and take in God's unwavering love.

This is how you invoke the love of your higher power. When you trust yourself and the Universe, you will feel immediate relief, not because the matter is solved but because you'll be able to finally release the physical tension in your body and relieve the anguish of holding everything inside.

You'll be able to finally put to rest any false stories that you may have told yourself.

- "If I own this mistake, I won't be loved."

- "If I talk about my feelings or childhood, I'm dishonoring my family."

- "If I admit to feeling pain, nobody will show up for me."

- "If I share my secrets, I will be judged."

- "If I talk about my fear, I will be labeled a weak person."

- "If I express my grief, I will fall apart."

- "If I admit to any shortcoming, I will be seen as unworthy."

All of these messages reinforce fear. Some people may even tell themselves they won't move forward unless they get an apology. Their entire future is attached to this idea that an apology is necessary. They think that they'll feel better once somebody feels shame for their wrongdoing. However, healing isn't about punishing the person who hurt us. It's about coming to terms with your feelings.

There's nothing that anyone can say or do to rectify pain if you are unwilling to meet yourself and process your emotions. It's that raw confrontation that frees you from the trauma. This is when you step out of being a victim, and you experience a profound shift in consciousness. It's empowering because you take back your energy and cut the emotional cord that has been attached to a person or emotional event in your life.

Your power shifts back to you when you release the attachment that someone owes you something or that someone else has to suffer. The truth is that your healing cannot be contingent on other people. We can become prisoners of those thoughts. It's not up to us to decide what the proper retribution for another person is. They will have to face their own conscience, karma, and consequences. This is why it's best to view your healing as a solitary process. You decide the terms of your growth, and the Universe will take care of the rest.

As long as you are waiting for an apology, you are essentially giving your power away, and you remain a victim. Now, it really doesn't matter what event it was that set you back emotionally; the chances that you will receive an apology, reparation, vindication, or some act of contrition is highly unlikely. Most things are just out of our human control. There are painful experiences that we may not ever find answers to, but it's our faith that gives us closure.

There is one aspect of healing that we have yet to talk about, and that is **"forgiveness."** Forgiveness has a lot of layers to it. It's acknowledging that something painful has happened. You come to terms with the fact that you were emotionally injured. It doesn't mean that you condone or agree with it … you just accept that it cannot be any different. It's about your internal process, and it doesn't require a single thing from another person.

Forgiveness is a spiritual decision, and it will set you free. When you set the intention to heal yourself and enact forgiveness, you leave all the traumatic events that you went through in the past instead of carrying them with you. It may be a very difficult step to take, but it is very possible to arrive at compassion for the person who hurt you. It requires you to see pain through God's lens, which is unconditional love.

Those who project pain are likely to have many open wounds and unresolved traumas. People who bully, judge, or hurt others typically learn that behavior. Of course, this doesn't give people a free pass, but it helps you understand why people reenact pain, trauma, and other dysfunctional behaviors. They haven't done their emotional or spiritual work, so their actions come from a place of turmoil and unworthiness.

When we step back from pain and observe it, we can take our personal feelings out of the experiences and see things much more clearly. Some people might even get to a place of gratitude. This happens once a person has done their inner work. They acknowledge their feelings, but they also extract some larger lesson or purpose from their painful experience. Once healing ensues and a person reaches another level of clarity, they may even refer to the offender as a teacher.

When time has passed and healing happens, the need to punish our aggressors goes away. One may even look back at their worst moments in life with compassion and understanding. It is very likely that the person who cheats on you will also teach you boundaries and standards, the person who abandons you will teach you to value loyalty and consistency, and the person who is ungrateful in your life will teach you the importance of verbalizing your love and appreciation.

Everything comes down to your willingness and openness to grow. If you can see beyond your pain, then you shall find something positive and redeeming about everything and everyone. This is the nature of spirituality and healing. It's maintaining unconditional love. As for the person who turns their painful experience into service, they are succeeding in their purpose because they have turned loss or sadness into something meaningful.

This chapter might be the hardest one to digest because we are choosing to take responsibility for our story, emotions, and well-being. We are letting go of the identification that we are victims. We also let go of the story that we aren't worthy of love, good health, joy, financial abundance, or positive relationships.

I opened up this chapter with my story about the loss of a tree. It may seem a little melodramatic to some, but here's the larger point. Healing is about coming to terms with ourselves and our truth. It's realizing that nothing can change what has already happened. Apologies may or may not come, but they do not hinder our healing process. We can only control ourselves, and we get to determine what follows: disappointment, grief, or trauma.

Pain is personal. It makes very little difference whether people get it or not. Our greatest challenge is to clear the emotional space for us to love again. You don't have to understand all the steps to redemption. You just have to be open to healing, and God will take it from there.

Stay Compassionate.

Love,

Krista

Personal Reflection

For this exercise, you will need a pen and your journal.

1) I invite you to close your eyes and think about the words "I'm sorry." Visualize the words on paper and then imagine hearing them. Is there somebody or some experience in your life in which you have been waiting for an apology?

2) Is there a specific person that you have felt anger or resentment toward? If so, who is that person and what is the pain that you have been holding in for so long? Keep in mind that this is just for you. Whatever you feel, write it down. You are giving voice to your raw emotions. Be as specific as you can and write until you feel like you've gotten everything out.

Now, take several slow, deep breaths and let what you wrote sink in.

3) I want to bring the moment back to you. Ask yourself if there is something or someone that you have been holding a grudge against. What was your role? Is it possible that you have been placing shame on yourself for something that happened a long time ago? Take a blank page from your journal and address a letter to yourself.

Dear _____,

*I'm sorry*_____

_____

_____

Love,

_____

From there, write down anything that you have been holding in or that you have been punishing yourself for. Write as much as you need to complete the exercise. Once you have finished writing, end the letter with these words:

"I may have gone through some very painful experiences, but they no longer hold me back from living my best life. Today, I release any guilt or shame that has been interfering with my well-being and happiness. I choose faith over fear. I am loved and supported."

Close your letter with your name. Take a moment to read your letter a few times and just notice what you feel. Has anything shifted for you? You might decide to keep this letter for a little while to read over again. When you are ready, you can burn and transmute the energy. As you release it, think about a compassionate message that you can give to yourself to reinforce healing and self-acceptance.

Chapter Nineteen

Grief Has a Gift

Throughout this book, I've made lots of references to grief. That means a lot of different things to different people. For that reason, I want to go there and break this topic wide open. I want to help you recognize what loss looks like and feels like. It goes well beyond the death of a loved one. It could represent the loss of a friendship, divorce, an empty nest, graduation, changing homes, loss of a pet, leaving a job, or some strange parting of ways. Any situation that asks you to "let go" can evoke grief.

When I initially finished writing this book, I was so relieved to cross the finish line, and yet I didn't feel that same elation that I felt with my previous books. I wasn't sure what was missing. During the next two nights, I tossed and turned; I couldn't sleep. I kept hearing the same message, **"You're not done yet. You left out a chapter."** I thought about what I was holding back, and then it became clear to me. I was carrying a lot of unresolved grief. I felt like God was asking me to sort through my aching heart and write about it.

Over the next couple of weeks, I embraced the challenge to do some personal work on myself. I didn't realize that I was still grieving the loss of my father and in-laws. I knew they were in a better place, but I missed them terribly. I also had a lot of feelings regarding my move to Arizona. While the decision has been positive, I missed amazing people and aspects of my life that were so comforting and rewarding.

Just days before our big move to Arizona, we found ourselves with positive Covid tests. My son Vince was leaving for the Navy, and I had to say goodbye from across the room. It was heart-wrenching. I remember sleeping in his room with his favorite blanket. I isolated myself and cried for the next two days.

Vince had pulled everything off the wall except a wooden rosary, and I found myself staring at it and wondering what that moment was teaching me. I was so burdened with heartache. I surrendered what I could in the moment, but I had some overwhelming feelings of punishment and despair.

I barely got to say goodbye to anybody. I felt like I was abandoning my family and a part of myself. Without proper hugs and in-person goodbyes, I felt a terrible void. It was grief. It was not easy, but I finally decided to honor those feelings that were packed up with all the boxes in the moving truck.

I tackled my feelings one by one and brought in as much love as possible, and I finally gave myself some time to feel those tangled emotions and untie the knots. I invited forgiveness into my heart, not because I regretted my decision to move but because I was carrying a lot of guilt and sadness. I hated being further away from my mother and the rest of my family.

We don't always equate goodbyes, graduations, leaving a job or a place that we lived for a long time with loss, but when you let go of something or someone that has been a big part of your life, grief is part of the process. I've learned that the older we get, the more goodbyes we experience. It does pose some very interesting questions about attachment. What is too much and what is too little?

As long as we feel love and devotion, we shall go through these intense losses. We can all agree: Love is the most magnificent part of being alive. When we open our hearts and say "yes" to love, we don't realize it at the moment, but we are also signing up for grief. There is no grief without love or love without grief. We just know that we're all in, and there's some illusion that it will last forever.

It's true that love plays out in the most glorious ways. It allows you to feel so many different emotions: excitement, passion, giddiness, joy, purpose, support, and gratitude. Eventually, something will come along and shift the dynamic of a relationship that seemed sturdy and unshakable. However simple or complicated, there's an abrupt ending, and you cannot escape the sadness. It's unimaginable that something so powerful has to end, so the heart feels intense pain.

It's unlikely that we all stay in the exact same place. Life will pull us in different directions. Sometimes, we outgrow people; other times they outgrow us, or the thing that brought you together has run its course. People may change their path because they follow their kids, change jobs, downsize, or retire. They might move for health reasons, financial reasons, or to live out some new adventure. The point is it's not personal.

Whether it's change or the loss of a loved one, life presents us with these gut-wrenching goodbyes, and that's why certain relationships have a season. Grief teaches us that change is inevitable and nothing is really ours except for the memories and growth. Grief makes us stronger, more compassionate, and more trusting. When nothing stays the same, grief takes you to the next level of preparedness and consciousness to let go of this life to be with God.

I know that most people don't think of it this way, but grief has a gift. We just have to be brave enough to sit with it and unpack it. I suppose that's where a lot of people run into trouble. They deny grief, avoid it, or replace it with some temporary Band-Aid. Whether it's putting in long hours at work, mindless shopping on the internet, drinking a bottle of wine, vegging out in front of the TV, or overindulging in comfort food, those are just temporary distractions so they don't have to deal with their loss.

This is why we need a spiritual perspective. It helps us see beyond the physical loss. If we only focus on what is gone, we cannot embrace all the good things waiting for us: every burden, personal adversity, disaster, crisis, or loss is an opportunity to go inward and become closer to God. Earlier in the book, I called it **"The Invitation."** I want you to know that death is an invitation too.

Death helps you understand that you have a flight plan. Grief is the healing process that many people want to bypass, but it teaches you more about yourself than any other experience. Nobody can tell you to walk through that door. You are the only person who can give yourself permission to feel your emotions.

There is no greater reminder for us to live more joyfully than to lose someone we love. I have found that there are some helpful questions that can assist you during your grieving process.

"Is it possible that God has a new plan for my life?"

"Has a new path or purpose opened up for me as a result of this loss?"

"Can I take some wisdom from this loss and become a better human being?"

"How does this mark some new beginning for me?"

"What is the gift that this experience offers to me?"

We may not see it right away, but what may initially appear as a tragic ending may place you in a new position to start over or serve a larger purpose. When we look at death through our limited human experience, we have little to compare it to. It's just one big, painful ending. However, once you look at death from a spiritual perspective, you shall see that death always prepares you for something else, and we really have no idea what plan God has in store for us.

When we look at death as a punishment, we miss the opportunity for expansion. When we only see loss as a period of suffering, we subconsciously refuse the possibility for blessings to exist. This speaks to the duality of life. Pain and love coexist in this physical world, and we are continuously invited to untangle our experiences and draw inspiration.

Without some spiritual context, we are likely to believe that we are alone in the grief process. Trust that God is guiding you through everything, and for those who have never leaned into their spirituality before, I have some very simple advice.

Place your hand over your heart, close your eyes, and breathe. Breathe slowly and deeply until you feel God's energy around you. Then, ask him to support you and get to the other side of your sadness. He will take it from there.

There isn't a single person who doesn't have grief tucked away somewhere in their body, and this chapter may be the one that frees you from sorrow, illness, or stuckness. Should you open yourself to your higher power and this healing process, you will find something kind and useful. You will find Grace. You see, grief is not about staying in a dark place. It is about seeing your life with love and light.

Recently, I was moved by a presentation about grief by Sunny

Dawn Johnston. Her perspective is a game changer. **"Death is the great equalizer. It makes you evaluate your life in a deeper way. There is polarity to everything. Without the investment of love, there is no grief. Death may cause us to initially tighten up and contract, but it's actually helping us to become more expansive."**

Death is always a shock, even if you know that a person has a fatal diagnosis or they are on Hospice care. It's typical to wish for more time together, but when the soul's journey is complete, we must deal with the finality of their physical body being gone forever. Most people get stuck on that part. However, there's another perspective that is far more extraordinary. We may no longer have their physical presence, but we can keep their spirit with us. It makes no difference if it is a parent, partner, son or daughter, sibling, distant relative, friend, dog, or cat. The soul carries on.

Before I dove into my spiritual education, I believed that death was this tragic ending, but I now understand that it's actually a whole new beginning. This shift in outlook came from studying the human condition and love. To be in love means that you are dedicated and invested in someone so much that you have an experience of godliness. When you align with that part of yourself that is sacred, you become selfless and joyful. Love allows you to experience joy, which is the highest frequency available. To be in a state of love is to experience God's greatest intention for you.

However delightful and fulfilling it all is, love comes with the harsh reality that people will die and leave us. Sometimes, death is sudden, accidental, or premature. It may be the result of a sickness, a fatal diagnosis, old age, or a long-standing battle with dementia. Love and loss are intermingled, and given the choice, most of us would do it all over again to experience just one more day with the person we love.

We know that the fear of death can be paralyzing, and so most people avoid all conversations that have to do with mortality. However, to be in denial or some state of oblivion changes the way you live. It's not uncommon for someone grieving to put up walls around their emotions or assume the role of **"the Strong One."** They may tell themselves they are doing it for their children or other family members, but it's just a survival mechanism, a form of self-protection.

We may tell ourselves that if we avoid our feelings long enough the pain will go away too, but that's not how grief works. It has a gift for you, and until you open it up, your heart cannot express itself fully, and you are likely to stagnate in your grieving process. This makes it impossible to move forward, and suddenly, you feel like a stranger in your own life.

It happened to me when my dad died, when my Nana passed away, and when a dear neighbor passed away after a long battle with cancer. It happened when my friend Leslie didn't wake up one morning. When death happens, most of us aren't prepared, and we fall into the emotional abyss known as grief. It's not only heartbreaking, it's traumatic. That's why you hear people say, **"I'm still in shock."** It knocks the wind out of you, and it takes you into survival mode, where you must protect yourself from any additional pain.

They say that grief is a visceral experience. That means that it's felt on the deepest human level as if it's inside the organs of the body. It bypasses all intellectual reasoning and logic. It evokes fear and the feeling of helplessness. The body goes into overload, and this is why you might see people freeze up, curl up in the fetal position, or shut down.

It would be insensitive of me to say that I know exactly how a person feels in their time of loss because it's very personal. However, I do know that death has a lot of the same characteristics as trauma. Trauma defies reasoning or logic, and it disrupts the nervous system. The exposure is so distressing it alters your body chemistry, and changes your view of yourself and the rest of the world. Trauma affects your mind, body, and spirit in such a way that you feel like you'll never be the same.

There isn't a single part of that description that doesn't also describe the experience of death. To lose someone you love means that you lose something in yourself too. It could be your innocence, joy, a sense of safety, a human bond, or the shared experience of working together, raising kids together, or being a part of a family circle. There was a time when I believed that death takes all that away, but I have released that narrow perspective. The memories are still ours to keep, and the person we've said goodbye to is still present in spiritual support.

It wasn't that long ago that I held a women's workshop in my home with Sunny, and we discussed death in great depth. My big takeaway from the night is that grief has its stages **(denial, anger, bargaining, depression, and acceptance)**, but the more we focus on the absence of a person, the less likely it is for us to expand or move forward. It lowers our frequency so far down that it cuts off the vital circulation of love. Without love we suffer.

Grief brings you closer to God: it also helps you connect with the other side, where you can feel the presence of angels and loved ones who have left the physical world. You won't be able to see signs or receive messages unless you are holding a higher vibration. This explains why people often experience their loved ones in dreams. There are no psychological restrictions or energetic barriers when we are in a dream state.

Remember that your loved ones will not drop their frequency to meet you where you are. Instead, you must raise your vibration to meet them. You can do this through stillness, prayer, breathwork, a walk in nature, meditation, writing in a journal, and placing your attention on emotions that have a higher frequency, like gratitude, joy, or love. Any ritual, mantra, or intention that brings you to the present moment will assist you in the grieving process because it will loosen up your tight grip.

If it's okay with you, I want to share a true story that brings this entire subject to life. About a month before my scheduled event on love and loss, I found myself in a whirlwind of grief. As I reflect on the events, I see the entire experience as divine timing. My husband and I were on a road trip to Sonoma County to see family and go to a wedding. Paul had a terrible cough that progressed with each day that passed. After a negative Covid test, he agreed that he should get a doctor's opinion.

We ended up in the emergency room. Five hours later, they said, "We will treat you for pneumonia, but your chest scan is pretty alarming. You should follow up with your doctor as there may be something more significant going on." The doctor used the "C word" several times. The possibility took my breath away. Well, that was just enough information to make a girl go crazy and think of grim scenarios. I found myself over the next week in some uncomfortable silence. I didn't know what to do with my feelings or my fear. If I'm being honest, my mind went to dark places.

It would take another week to get in to see a doctor at home, and even though I had no information to confirm any true diagnosis, I felt incredibly scared; my body was contracted, my nervous system was frazzled, and I noticed that I held my breath a lot. I literally went through all the same physical and emotional responses that one goes through when one experiences a traumatic loss.

There is a name for this. It's called **"Anticipatory Grief."** You go through grief before anything actually happens. You run through these scenarios in which you give up the person that you love. You do all the things that you would do if you suddenly lost your loved one. You collapse in shock, you get angry and bargain with God, you drop your frequency, and you pray that you find some miracle or life preserver.

Here's what eventually came about. Paul and I agreed to lean into our spirituality and talk about how we felt. Everything shifted once we agreed to get honest about our emotions. We realized that the lifeline that we were looking for was God. This seemed to echo the message that my mother-in-law, Cathy, experienced in the hospital. We now had our own experience of **"Redemptive Suffering."**

Eventually, we will all be faced with a personal trial that requires us to surrender our pain to God. The Universe will determine when it's time to let go. We can resist it and fight it, but we cannot change the fact that all experiences have an ending, and all of us will cross over to the other side. The sooner we integrate that wisdom, the easier it is to hold space for Grace.

It was a few weeks later that we learned that Paul had a tricky case of Valley Fever. That news gave us relief and following that entire experience we found ourselves spiritually stronger than ever. If you were to ask me why all that happened, I think it was an awakening of some sort, where we were asked to trust our faith and one another.

If I didn't have certain spiritual tools in place, I believe that I would have stayed in that dark place much longer than I did. Fear told me one story and faith told me a different one. I love that we prayed together, played scrabble to pass the time, and we asked ourselves what good can come from this entire experience.

As I look back on that moment, I feel like I was supposed to go through grief because it gave me a deeper understanding of life and compassion. It drew me closer to God and my husband and allowed me to experience the intense feelings associated with loss. The experience was profound and enlightening. We may not be able to choose when something comes to an end, but we are never without choice. Grief is just another fork in the road where we must decide between love or fear.

At the end of the day, I think that God placed me in a unique position to document Cathy's experience. He also granted me an experience to unravel grief in a very personal way. I now have the wisdom to recognize grief in myself and others, and I can now write about loss in a meaningful way. Anytime you see pain up close, you are likely to take away incredible insight.

As we wrap up this chapter on grief, I want to highlight a few takeaways:

> **We cannot resist change or death.**
>
> **We are never alone in our grief.**
>
> **Love, loss, and death are intermingled.**
>
> **Grief assists us in our spiritual wisdom and transformation.**
>
> **Once you lean into your spirituality, the fear goes away.**
>
> **Your loved ones are still in your life, but you must get present to feel them.**

This is a handy list, but you are the one who ultimately decides how to manage grief. I just advise that you remain open and inquisitive. Be patient with yourself and loosen up your tight grip on your emotions and the things in your life that have run their natural course. It is when you trust God and invite Grace into your heart that you stop questioning the time and order of loss.

And so it is.

Stay Flexible.

Love,

Krista

Questions & Reflection

This is the time to pull out your journal. During this chapter, I invited you to think about a few questions that relate to loss in your life. In order to do this more thoroughly, I want to invite you to give grief a name. This may refer to the death of a loved one or possibly a pet. It may be a severed relationship, or it might be some big change in your life where you are readjusting your identity. Consider the possibility that grief has a gift for you. Take time to go through these questions one at a time. Once you are done, notice if you feel any different about this particular loss.

1) What would you say is the most difficult thing for you to let go of right now?

2) Could it be that God has a new plan for your life? If so, what might that be?

3) Has a new path or purpose opened up for you as a result of this loss?

4) What wisdom will you take away from this experience to become a better human being?

5) What is the gift that grief has for you?

Chapter Twenty

I AM ...

*I*t's incredible how shifting the focus back to spirituality liberates us from fear, distractions, and trauma. There are just way too many of us who are beating ourselves up over something that happened years ago, carrying around family guilt, absorbing fear from society, and clenching onto grief.

When you no longer know what it feels like to be yourself anymore, then it's best to find a still place and put your hand over your heart. Ask yourself, "What part of my body is trying to get my attention? What part of my story needs acceptance? Which problem needs compassion or forgiveness?" The only way to restore your freedom is to cut those negative cords that obstruct the flow of energy and love.

That high vibrational energy that we all seek can be found in the affirming words, **"I AM."** It essentially means that you are in sync with your truth, values, purpose, health, and divinity, and you see yourself in a position to grow at all times. "I AM" is that sacred energy that links you to your inner guidance. It is your strength and confidence, and it holds Grace and gentle support for you at all times.

"I AM" keeps us grounded in our personal values, but it also acknowledges our collective priorities. There is an African term that celebrates this very same philosophy. It is called "**Ubuntu,**" which means that we are being human through other people. Ubuntu recognizes that we all have a greater responsibility to ourselves, society, and humanity. It is a way of being, **"I AM what I AM because of who we all are."**

Most people would agree that there is a lack of empathy and tolerance in the world right now. The world is losing common ground. The spirit of "I AM" could very well put us back on track. This spiritual perspective not only invites all of us to expand our consciousness and take responsibility for our health and choices, but also invest in ideas, solutions, and experiences that are in the highest good for all humankind.

When you hold this awareness for yourself and others, you assume another level of responsibility for the earth and human progress. I call this **"Spiritual Integration."** This means that all experiences inside yourself and in the world are just advancing you further along in your personal transformation and elevating our collective consciousness.

Spiritual integration is about holding integrity and abiding by a higher code of ethics and behavior. Maya Angelou's quote speaks to this wisdom, **"Do the best you can until you know better. Then, when you know better, do better."** It encourages you to see everything in terms of growth, healing, and forward progress. It's a mindset that reinforces solidarity and celebrates collaboration, **"We are in this together."** It strengthens faith and good character and helps us understand that our collective progress relies on our self-improvement.

"I AM" offers stability. It holds space for both masculine and feminine energies, which provide a much more balanced perspective. The divine feminine is associated with receptiveness, intuition, collaboration, and patience. It is nurturing, healing, gentle, emo-

tional, flexible, creative, expressive, and wise. The divine masculine is oriented toward logic, reason, and decisive action. It is characterized by strength, discipline, and leadership.

When these two energies are married together, the human spirit
can soar to brand-new heights. I first learned about "I AM" from
a spiritual teacher named Emmanual Daugher. I was on a retreat
in Sedona for my 50th birthday. I can remember how simple and
profound his explanation was. He referred to it as **"Being
Awake."** Spirit leads us through trials not to break us but to elevate our consciousness and restore balance to our inner self and
outer world.

Most people haven't heard that perspective, so they view their
burdens as some sort of downfall … a collapse in protection, trust,
love, health, and morality. However, "I AM" is about restoration.
It is a soulful journey back to yourself in which you allow space
for divinity and human frailty. It is a brave pilgrimage in which a
person searches for moral significance and belonging. While this
is a solitary journey, it creates an amazing ripple effect.

"I AM" will honor every arduous passage that you go through.

"I AM a survivor."

"I AM in recovery."

"I AM courageous."

"I AM resilient."

"I AM imperfect."

"I AM broken."

"I AM lost."

"I AM in discovery."

"I AM alone."

"I AM grieving."

"I AM changing."

"I AM growing."

"I AM starting over."

I remember a few years back when our nonprofit, "The Fabulous Women," put on a retreat for women. We had grandmothers, mothers, and teenagers participate in the day. It was fabulous because we talked about how all of us, despite our age differences, had something quite vulnerable in common. We often feel intimidated by all the pressure from society **"to be more, have more, and do more."** We all agreed that it's overwhelming to take on everybody else's expectations because it interferes with our confidence and peace of mind.

That pressure is the product of conditioning from family, society, and media. Regardless of its origin, all of the women from that day agreed that we must turn our insecurity into self-love and manage our energy and mental health. When the forces outside of us are louder than our inner voice, then we become susceptible to stress, drama, chaos, anxiety, and dysfunctional habits.

We came to terms with a troubling reality: we simply cannot meet everyone's expectations and also abide by our own inner guidance. It's just not possible. It's when we allow everyone else to define who we are that we lose our true selves. This is when inner conflict sets in, and spirituality takes a back seat to fear.

We began our human journey with wholeness and possibility. Then society comes in and breaks us down into smaller groups and pieces and tells us that we aren't good enough, successful enough, pretty enough, smart enough, thin enough, etc. Every woman from that workshop expressed some sadness that she had lost a part of herself. The noise from the world had become too loud.

Well, we did something very cool that day. We painted the words "I AM" down our arms with black paint, and then we filled in the blank.

I saw 70-year-old women with powerful messages:

"I AM BEAUTIFUL."

"I AM WISE."

I saw middle-aged moms with bold declarations:

"I AM STRONG."

"I AM WORTHY."

"I AM PEACEFUL."

I saw teenagers with brave affirmations:

"I AM KIND."

"I AM LOVE."

"I AM UNSTOPPABLE!"

Yes, something amazing happened on that day. Those women took their power back. They got in touch with their hearts and that part of themselves that is whole and spiritual. Instead of concentrating on defects, they focused on their gifts and goodness. Self-compassion flowed to places that were otherwise blocked by fear, expectations, and judgment.

If you were to ask me what it was that came alive for those women on that day, I would say that it was self-love. They reconnected with their Grace and divinity and put fear in its proper place. It's amazing how common this is for all of us. We forget just how resourceful, powerful, loveable, and resilient we already are.

The most critical piece to your healing is realizing that you must silence that inner critic that tells you that you're not good enough or strong enough. When you quiet that voice that undermines your strength and devalues your existence, then those feelings of unworthiness go away.

"I AM" is empowering because you get to define your experience and insert positive messages that propel your life forward. You can add any word that you need to boost your spirit, elevate your confidence, or invite healing into your body. For instance, "I am loved and supported" provides a renewed focus for any situation. It reinforces that everything is going to be okay and that you're not alone.

When you know your true value, then you can take back your life. That's when you also listen to your inner guidance instead of piling on the fear of a mixed-up world. Some people joke that it would have been nice if we came into this world with a handbook filled with instructions. Once I started healing myself, I realized that the manual that everyone is looking for is spirituality. God is giving us messages all the time, but we're just too damn stressed, busy, and fearful to notice.

Faith provides you with a manual for self-care and replenishment.

It teaches you how to pick yourself up after a trauma, how to surrender what is out of your control, how to maintain loving relationships, and how to find forgiveness and fulfillment. It helps you build social confidence and body confidence, and it allows you to trust the order in which things come and go from your life. It helps you realize that you have a choice of what you allow into your thoughts and energetic field.

This presents the perfect segue to introduce you to the seven main spiritual energy centers in your body. They are called **"chakras."** They represent levels of consciousness. They hold the truth. Chakras are energy points, and learning about them will increase your awareness of the relationship between your mind, body, and spirit. There are different characteristics to these seven chakras, but they all tap into your inner knowing.

The first time I learned about the chakras was when I had a beautiful Reiki healer named Bevin Fulton come to my women's group. I later got my certification in Reiki from Sunny Dawn Johnston who reinforced my understanding of energy. Bevin talked about these energy fields in great detail. I was mesmerized by her explanation. I took massive notes because the information was so empowering. As you become familiar with these energy fields, you can determine whether a chakra is underactive or overactive.

The goal is to maintain some internal balance so that you can feel more at ease. By isolating a chakra, you can figure out where there are possible conflicts in your body and your life. These energetic blocks may represent unresolved grief or trauma, suppressed feelings, or physical manifestations. These sensitive energy centers will impact the efficiency of your body systems and greatly influence the way you give and reserve energy.

Each chakra has an approximate resonant vibration, which translates to light and frequency range. This creates beautiful hues of color. When these chakras are healthy and working together, they serve as a holistic system that keeps the body balanced. When the chakras are out of alignment, they get tied up in energetic knots. Those knots could be **emotional** (unexpressed feelings), **mental** (negative thought patterns), **physical** (injuries, illness, wounds), or **spiritual** (some energetic imprint from your soul or another that interferes with your field and causes conflict).

So, what does it mean to have healthy chakras? Well, it refers to the body's ability to maintain physical and subtle body functions at high levels of homeostasis. This is why your emotional well-being is so critical to your body's performance. If you are carrying sadness, anger, stress, or grief, the chakras are likely to be blocked or compromised in some way.

These emotional entanglements will cause distortion and disrupt the flow of energy coming and going. It will affect your immunity and prevent you from accessing higher vibrational emotions like love, joy, peace, and enlightenment. When you consider all the energy and information that we are processing on a daily basis, it's no wonder that we often feel tangled up in stress. Instead of feeling overwhelmed by the enormity of life, we can literally address our needs much more specifically by surveying each chakra center.

Healing helps you calibrate at a higher bandwidth of energy. This is when you feel harmonious. Aside from the physical and emotional benefits, healing raises your psychic ability. Synchronicities tend to happen way more often. This opens the spiritual portal where magical things come together, and you attract positive people, opportunities, and blessings. This is when you know that you are in the flow and aligned with the Universe.

I want to emphasize that I am literally just scratching the surface of the explanation of chakras. Should you feel extra curious or compelled to go deeper in your understanding of these spiritual energy centers, there are plenty of books that are exclusively dedicated to this subject. I found an amazing book about chakras by April Pfender. It's called *The Complete Guide to Chakras … Activating the 12-Chakra Energy System For Balance and Healing.*

For the purpose of keeping this subject easy to digest, I have taken information from her book and my course work with Bevin Fulton and Sunny Dawn Johnston to create a simple description of the chakras. This will allow you to identify the personality, characteristics, and benefits of chakra centers. Chakra healing is absolutely transformative. Once you know what these chakras represent in your body, it opens the door to another level of healing.[19]

I will be identifying basic concepts about chakras:

- The name of each chakra and the affirmation associated with it

- The location of the chakra in the body

- The healing color associated with the chakra

- Signs of an overactive or underactive chakra

- Affirmations to balance the chakra

- Stones that support the chakra

---

[19] April Pfender, "The Complete Guide to Chakras…Activating the 12-Chakra Energy System For Balance and Healing," Rockridge Press, June 2022, pgs. 1-28, 73-154.

THE ROOT CHAKRA: "I Am"

CHARACTERISTICS: Self-Preservation, Basic Trust, Grounding, Stability, Foundation.

LOCATION: It is located at the base of the spine which is between our reproductive organs and the perineum.

COLOR: The Root is the first Chakra. It is represented by the color ruby red, which invokes feelings of passion and power. Red is the color of love and desire.

UNDERACTIVE CHAKRA: Passive, apathetic, disconnected to body, unsettled, poor focus and discipline, exhausted and spacey, notably underweight, fearful, anxious, and restless, may have a difficult time setting boundaries.

OVERACTIVE CHAKRA: intense feeling of lack, not having enough, or being enough, which can lead to self-indulgent behaviors like hoarding and overeating, may be seen as lazy, sluggish, or materialistic.

ENERGETIC BLOCKS: Deals with survival/blocked by fear.

AFFIRMATIONS TO RESTORE BALANCE: I AM safe and secure, I AM in full trust of the Universe to support me, I AM right where I need to be, I AM confident that everything happens with divine timing and order, I AM independent, strong, and resilient, I AM living an abundant life where all my needs are met.

SUPPORTIVE STONES: Red Coral, Red/Brown Jasper, Black Obsidian, Tourmaline & Garnet.

THE SACRAL CHAKRA: "I Feel"

CHARACTERISTICS: Self-Gratification, Emotions, Sexuality, Relationships, Joy, Intimacy, Connection.

LOCATION: It is located two inches below the navel.

COLOR: The Sacral is the second Chakra. It is represented by the color orange, which invokes creativity, playfulness, sexuality, and innovation.

UNDERACTIVE CHAKRA: Social and childhood conditioning plays into their rigid beliefs, low or nonexistent sex drive, lacks desire, passion, self-confidence, and excitement, insecure, poor social skills, and denies themselves pleasure.

OVERACTIVE CHAKRA: Addicted to sex, ruled by emotions, uses seduction to manipulate others, severe mood swings, obsessive attachments, self-indulgent, often seen as insincere or superficial.

ENERGETIC BLOCKS: Deals with pleasure/blocked by guilt.

AFFIRMATIONS TO RESTORE BALANCE: I FEEL beautiful, I AM allowing myself to enjoy pleasure, I AM a sexual being, I AM passionate about life, I AM in love with my body, I AM sensual and creative.

SUPPORTIVE STONES: Carnelian, Orange Calcite, Citrine, Sun Stone & Tiger's Eye.

SOLAR PLEXUS CHAKRA: "I Do"

CHARACTERISTICS: Self-Definition, Energy, Vitality, Wisdom, Desire, Power.

LOCATION: It is located at the base of the sternum just above the navel.

COLOR: The Solar Plexus is the third Chakra. It is represented by the color yellow. It's bright like the sun. It is the color of joy, inspiration, and happiness. It awakens inner vitality. It invokes confidence, power, and strength.

UNDERACTIVE CHAKRA: Low energy, unreliable, weak-minded, anxious, difficulty staying present, low self-confidence, lack of self-discipline, fear of rejection, victim mentality.

OVERACTIVE CHAKRA: Out of alignment, overly aggressive, dominant, controlling, egotism, competitive, power hungry, stubborn, may display perfectionism.

ENERGETIC BLOCKS: Deals with willpower/blocked by shame.

AFFIRMATIONS TO RESTORE BALANCE: I DO my best at all times, I AM strong and confident, I AM directing my life experiences, I AM true to myself, I AM worthy of abundance, I AM inspired and empowered.

SUPPORTIVE STONES: Citrine, Pyrite, Amber, Sun Stone, Agate, Tiger's Eye & Calcite.

THE HEART CHAKRA: "I Love"

CHARACTERISTICS: Self-Love, Hope, Compassion, Healing.

LOCATION: It is located in the center of the chest between the breast bone in the rib cage and between the lungs.

COLOR: The Heart is the fourth Chakra. It is represented by the color emerald green, which is the frequency of renewal, harmony, nature, and growth. The secondary color is pink, which invokes feelings of universal love, affection, intimacy, and compassion.

UNDERACTIVE CHAKRA: Emotionally shut down, fears relationships and intimacy, abandonment issues, prone to loneliness and depression, difficulty in forming and staying in relationships, lacking in self-love, antisocial, defensive, bitter, often seen as a victim.

OVERACTIVE CHAKRA: Codependent, clingy, lack of boundaries, jealous, demanding, people-pleaser, does things at the expense of self, loss of identity.

ENERGETIC BLOCKS: Deals with love/blocked by grief.

AFFIRMATIONS TO RESTORE BALANCE: I LOVE myself, I AM loved, I AM attracting healthy and fulfilling relationships, I AM fearless, I AM open to receive love, I AM open to give love freely, I AM grateful for my family and friends.

SUPPORTIVE STONES: Rose Quartz, Adventurine, Green Jade, Amazonite, & Green Opal.

THE THROAT CHAKRA: "I Speak"

CHARACTERISTICS: Self-Expression, Communication, Creativity, Healing.

LOCATION: It is located at the base of the throat.

COLOR: The Throat is the fifth Chakra. It is represented by all shades of blue. Blue is associated with integrity, depth, stability, balance, loyalty, and intelligence. The frequency is calm and serene. It invokes security and trust.

UNDERACTIVE CHAKRA: Afraid to speak up and so it causes turmoil and physical manifestations (sore throat, laryngitis, coughing, stuttering), difficulty expressing emotions, weak voice.

OVERACTIVE CHAKRA: Talks too much, unable to listen, defensive, interrupts conversations, gossips, prone to lying, judgmental, arrogant, rude, may take on compulsive behaviors like overeating, jaw clenching, or teeth grinding.

ENERGETIC BLOCKS: Deals with truth/blocked by lies.

AFFIRMATIONS TO RESTORE BALANCE: I SPEAK my truth, I AM in alignment with my personal values, I AM safe to express myself, I AM able to communicate my feelings and needs with Grace and Ease.

SUPPORTIVE STONES: Turquoise, Tanzanite, Lapis, Lazuli, Amazonite & Kyanite.

THE THIRD EYE: "I See"

CHARACTERISTICS: Self-Reflection, Awareness, Intuition, Insight, Psychic & Sensory Sight.

LOCATION: It is located an inch above the center of the eyebrows.

COLOR: The Third Eye is the sixth Chakra. It is represented by indigo and violet. The colors invoke spirituality, self-awareness, and reflection. The primary color, indigo, conveys integrity, devotion, and justice. As a secondary color, violet carries a frequency of dignity, sensitivity, and intuition.

UNDERACTIVE CHAKRA: lacks imagination and clarity, insensitive, moody, low self-confidence, difficulty seeing anything beyond one's frame of reference, attracts chaos, easily deceived, uses denial as a coping mechanism.

OVERACTIVE CHAKRA: Fantasizes about life being different, overthinking, obsessive, has difficulty concentrating, trouble connecting to inner desires.

ENERGETIC BLOCKS: Deals with insight/blocked by illusion.

AFFIRMATIONS TO RESTORE BALANCE: I SEE everything clearly, I AM wise and intuitive, I AM connected to my life's purpose, I AM open to receiving wisdom from others, I AM in full trust of the Universe, I AM calm.

SUPPORTIVE STONES: Lapis, Sapphire, Lazuli, Amethyst, Celestite, Labradorite & Obsidian.

CROWN CHAKRA: " I Know"

CHARACTERISTICS: Self-Knowledge, Spirituality, Understanding, Enlightenment, Cosmic Consciousness.

LOCATION: It is located at the top of the head.

COLOR: The Crown Chakra is the seventh chakra. It is said to contain all colors of the rainbow, and so it is denoted by the color white, which represents purity, light, and hope. The secondary color is violet, which is considered dynamic. This color is associated with spirituality, creativity, and mystery.

UNDERACTIVE CHAKRA: Separation of consciousness, spiritual cynicism, rigid belief system, difficulty learning, sensitive, loneliness, and lack of belonging.

OVERACTIVE CHAKRA: Overthinking, obsessive, feelings of superiority, inability to decide the smallest decisions, often confused and depressed.

ENERGETIC BLOCKS: Deals with cosmic energy/blocked by attachments.

AFFIRMATIONS TO RESTORE BALANCE: I KNOW what I need, I AM part of the divine, I AM connected to everything and everyone, I AM love and light, I AM at peace, I AM infinite and limitless.

SUPPORTIVE STONES: Clear Quartz, Moonstone, Amethyst, Labradorite, Howlite & Selenite.

There are so many different ways to approach your health. You rarely hear people say, **"I'm taking the day off to clear my chakras."** However, it's very impactful to your well-being. I have provided a number of "I AM" affirmations that you can incorporate into your self-care. You can also explore other modalities like Reiki, yoga, meditation, crystals, breathwork, swimming, prayer, horse therapy, nutrition, journaling, drawing, therapy, bodywork, herbal baths, hiking, exercise, smudging, music, and shaking and dancing. These modalities may be used individually or combined.

There's no debate. When your chakras are clear, you can tackle life with more Grace and Ease. That is an ongoing challenge because human beings absorb so much fear from one another, social media, news, technology, and political groups. Just remember that even if you're sensitive to other people's energies, you cannot just take on their moods or beliefs without your permission. You get to decide what comes in and out of your field.

My intention for this chapter was to help you see how sophisticated your body is in regulating energy and be able to discern between higher frequencies and lower frequencies. Healing is about the reclaiming of self, where you honor your heart, feelings, and entire story and remove any emotional debris that interferes with your heart. When you stand in your truth and power, then you shall open yourself up to the most extraordinary possibilities ever imagined.

Stay Awake.

Love,

Krista

Exercise & Reflection[20]

Allow 15-20 minutes.

This next segment is a powerful movement exercise. We are trying to awaken the body. As you shake and dance, you are likely to feel revitalized. You might notice a shift in your energy or attitude. Be open to all possibilities as you move. We are just opening up the chakras.

PART 1: The first step in this exercise is to find a safe place to move. You may want to choose a private place so that you can move freely without any interference or judgment. You are going to shake your body for 3:49 minutes.

I have provided a YouTube link to pull up on your phone or laptop. This song is arranged and sung by Emmanuel Daugher: YouTube.com/watch?v=vvZxGEF6Dj0

Enjoy the movement.

During the exercise, allow your head, arms, legs, and hips to move as much as you can. If you have health limitations, just do what is safe and comfortable. Plant your feet firmly on the ground at shoulder's width apart. Bend your knees slightly, and relax your shoulders and your breath. If you have physical limitations and need to hold onto something to avoid falling, please take care of yourself. Shake safely and to the best of your ability. Some people close their eyes during this exercise, or you can keep a soft gaze on the floor. Slow down or stop as needed. The goal is to continuously move your body for the duration of the song. Remember that you cannot do this incorrectly.

---

[20] This movement exercise was adapted from my Mind-Body Medicine training. I have changed the music to celebrate the music compositions of Emmanuel Daugher who inspired this chapter.

PART 2: Take a couple of breaths before you do the next segment. Notice how you feel in your body. For this next piece, you will move your body more gently for 3:17 minutes.

I have provided a YouTube link to pull up on your phone or laptop. This instrumental piece is arranged by Emmanuel Daugher:

emmanueld.s3.us-west-1.amazonaws.com/Goddess+Rising+Activation.mp3

Enjoy the movement.

PART 3: Once you are done with the movement, take out your journal and write down anything that you are experiencing in your body right now. Consider a few questions:

Did you notice a difference between the two types of songs?

Did you experience any resistance?

Did it get easier as time went on?

Did any memories come into your mind?

Did you connect with any emotion?

Do you have any new aspirations?

Chapter Twenty-One

Long Story Short ...

I feel very proud of the work that we've been doing together. We've slowly dismantled the narrative that healing is just for people who are sick, fragile, grieving, depressed, poor, disenfranchised, or weak. It's for you, it's for me, and anyone who is navigating through this thing we call **"life."** Our journey presents us with so many amazing experiences to go deeper in our understanding of ourselves, humanity, and spirituality, and the most important question that you can ask yourself is whether you're all in or not.

I suppose there are a million things we could do to improve this world together, but the most powerful decision that you can make is to take care of the stress in your life and honor your emotional needs. No matter how messy or complicated life is, your experiences are taking you further along in your transformation. It's incredible what happens when you step into your healing. Love is restored to all those places that have otherwise felt heavy or empty.

It's not uncommon for us to get overwhelmed by adversity, but I want to challenge you to see that moment as an opportunity to shift ... shift a position, a belief, a relationship, or a habit. Here is something that you may not have considered. The Universe is bringing you to a particular experience because it trusts that you are ready to push through another barrier to elevate your consciousness.

We know that transformation doesn't happen on vacation or those mundane days when you're at home on the couch watching Netflix. Nope, it happens when something disrupts your comfort zone. There are some elements of pain and discomfort that have to be addressed emotionally and spiritually. In those moments, you are tested to go beyond your limits. It requires massive courage. Here's the reality. Sometimes, we rise to the occasion, and other times, we collapse under the pressure.

According to Dragana Djukic, "Courage is something that everybody wants, yet courage is not just physical bravery. In general, there are six types of courage we may need to face life challenges":

1. Physical courage—Feeling fear yet choosing to act. Involves bravery at the risk of bodily harm or death and developing physical strength, resilience, and awareness.

2. Emotional courage—Following our heart. Opens us to feeling the full spectrum of emotions—pleasant and unpleasant—without attachment.

3. Intellectual courage—Expanding our horizons, letting go of the familiar. It is about our willingness to learn, unlearn, and re-learn with an open and flexible mind.

4. Social courage—To be yourself in the face of adversity. Involves the risk of social embarrassment or exclusion, unpopularity or rejection. It also involves leadership.

5. Moral courage—Standing up for what is right. Involves doing the right thing even when it is uncomfortable or unpopular.

6. Spiritual courage—Facing pain with dignity or faith. It helps us live with purpose and meaning through a heart-centered approach toward all life and oneself.[21]

Courage is largely determined by our willingness to trust ourselves and God. More often than not, we fall apart because we are afraid to change. We like our lives, and facing the unknown scares the shit out of us. There's comfort in predictability, and by the way, it makes no difference whether our lifestyle is healthy or dysfunctional; we get used to being in certain roles, and we don't like to steer too far from what we know.

Any disruption to your home, health, routine, or relationships is an invitation to reevaluate those old habits and patterns. Now, you've probably heard the saying, **"You can't teach an old dog new tricks."** That's true if you're dealing with a person who is committed to just ONE way of being. However, if they can set aside their ego, lean into their faith, and reflect on how they can become a better person, they might actually surprise themselves and see that change isn't so scary after all.

Over the years, I've heard many spiritual teachers talk about how important it is to **"Trust the process."** The reason this is such powerful advice is because you are choosing to focus on your spiritual support. When you apply faith to an obstacle, you are making an agreement to collaborate with the Universe. Rather than trying to control the outcome, you remain open to all blessings and possibilities.

It's true that some people might spend their entire lives circumventing healing just to avoid discomfort. The rationale is pretty simple. **"As long as I don't appear weak or admit to any grief**

---

[21] Dragana Djukic, "The Six Types of Courage," QuantumKoan, December 16, 2020, https://www.quantumkoan.com/the-six-types-of-courage/.

or dysfunction, then I can keep going on doing the same thing." Well, here's something to consider. **"What if you're not supposed to keep doing the same thing? What if God is trying to slow you down, help you get healthier, or get you out of a situation that isn't good for you?"**

We may be selling ourselves short when we avoid problems for the simple fact that we are quite resourceful. We underestimate our faith and resilience. More importantly, we simply don't know what is waiting for us on the other side of a storm. Ironically, emotional storms are no different than physical storms. There is a brief cleansing that takes place in order for new blessings to enter. The sight of a rainbow is proof that good things can follow a storm.

Most of us think our time here on Earth is a very linear experience. However, your purpose for being here is much more expansive. Long story short, your emotional well-being not only affects your health and your immediate circle, but it elevates the entire collective known as humanity. That's right! Your authenticity, self-care, self-love, morality, and kindness leave an energetic footprint on this world.

The reason that society has struggled so much is because we are trying to see everything through a tiny lens. We only take into account how things affect us individually. However, if you look at life from a spiritual perspective, then you will see God's larger vision in which we all benefit and thrive. The more people who win, the better off we all are! Spirituality takes a communal approach in which decisions are made from a position of wholeness, wellness, and oneness.

When you focus on spirituality, you essentially become the physical embodiment of peace and love. Earlier, I called it a **"lighthouse,"** and it's because your light shines so bright that you can affect people in the most meaningful ways. It elevates the vibration in your home, friend groups, workplace, church, neighborhood, and community. This is not exclusive to any one person. We all have the potential to become amazing leaders.

You just never know how your journey can motivate others. You might be the one who demonstrates courage and resilience to someone suffering, or you could be the reason that someone comes out of their shell or expresses their passion and creativity. That's right! You have the potential to open the door for somebody else seeking healing, and I find that rather inspiring.

Imagine that for a second. How incredibly rewarding it would be to influence the quality of life based on one criteria ... **LOVE**. We keep searching for significance and Grace, and yet it is already right in front of us. We've just allowed fear, distractions, and chaos to come between ourselves and God. I'll say out loud what many people are afraid to admit, **"Spirituality is what's missing from today's world."**

We cannot go through this life without greater consideration of God and others. Our entire human journey is about something bigger. It's bigger than you, and it's bigger than me, and it goes well beyond our physical appearance, possessions, and survival. It's about our spiritual development. Our well-being relies on collective consciousness.

I'm referring to:

the unraveling,

the self-discovery,

the acknowledgment of pain and grief,

the shedding,

the crying,

the healing,

the replenishment of self,

the renewal of faith,

the pursuit of knowledge,

the human bond,

the energetic exchange between ourselves, nature, and animals,

the expression of love,

and the impact that one awakened spirit can have on this world.

Yes, life is all these things and so much more. You have infinite potential. Oh, I know it's upsetting to see how certain aspects of the world are harsh, offensive, and stressful. I also know that it can be depressing to look at all the different problems all at once, but here's what you must hold onto. **God isn't asking you to heal everything ... JUST YOURSELF!**

When you evolve, everything else deepens: your passion, wisdom, purpose, joy, creativity, and relationships. It takes on the characteristics of a beautiful ivy that grows in the garden. It literally takes off in places that are unexpected and surprising.

Healing reinforces your best qualities, and just in case you have forgotten what that looks like in yourself, I want to remind you that the human spirit is brave, courageous, generous, and kind. **Healing is the single most important decision that you can make right now because you are not only taking care of your own needs, but you are putting LOVE back into the world.**

So, here's where you have an important decision to make. You can be a part of the movement to bring in more love and positive energy, or you can be part of the chaos and accept fear as a way of life. Either way, the world goes on. However, your role could be instrumental in improving family dynamics, elevating the morale at your job, or supporting your community in some meaningful way.

Historically, it just takes a couple of change-makers to have a massive influence on the culture of the world. There is a powerful quote by Gloria Steinem that says, **"The final stage of healing is using what happens to you to help other people."** Perhaps you have never really thought of adversity in this way, but if you look back at problems that you persevered through, you're also likely to identify another situation in your life in which you helped someone in their time of need.

Our time on earth is **NOT** as individualized as we once believed. Everything we do or say is either helping or diminishing the human collective. When you ask yourself if there is something good that can come from healing, consider God's greater vision. We are all here to love and support one another. I challenge you to see your growth as a circular blessing. Your spiritual investment will not only benefit your life and the people around you, but it will support a positive vision for humanity.

Long story short …

It's LOVE!

Stay Selfless.

Love,

Krista

Questions & Reflection

Let's explore the concept of healing further. If you accept the premise, **"It's not all about you,"** then it suggests that your healing can have some positive impact on others. This is a great time to pull out your journal. Think about something very challenging in your life. Give it a name. Is it a problem, symptom, trauma, feeling, or conflict?

Part 1: Once you have a name, ask yourself why this situation feels so personal and upsetting to you. Write down as much as you need to. Allow everything to come out with raw honesty. It's important that you do not edit your thoughts or feelings.

Part 2: For this next question, I want you to look at that same problem through a different lens. What spiritual purpose do you think this situation can have once you have healed from the inside out? Who could you serve, or what cause could you support? Could there be some greater benefit that you may not have considered before?

Part 3: Take a moment to compare the two answers that you just wrote down. How are they different? Does God have a takeaway for you from this exercise? Has the fact that you have been taking your problem personally stood in the way of your healing and greater purpose?

Chapter Twenty-Two

"I Want Something More"

There's a song by Pink that brings tears to my eyes every time I hear it on the radio. It's called **"A Million Dreams."** There's something about the lyrics that reminds me that everything is possible for me ... for you ... and for the world if we just believe in ourselves a little bit more. It's my greatest hope that people never lose sight of their talent or dreams.

I've often asked myself, **"What would it take for people to step into that magical mindset?"** The truth is that we can't access our dreams or joyful thinking if we are holding on for dear life. If your thoughts are consumed by stress, fear, and heavy things from your past, then you lose sight of all the wondrous things that you can experience in this lifetime.

There are so many compelling reasons to step into your healing. Being able to access your dreams may, in fact, be at the top of the list. Every time you take away a lesson from a difficult experience, you expand your knowledge, clarify what's important to you, and create a little more room for magic. This is the nature of healing. You release the darkest parts of your story so you can bring in more light.

Healing doesn't make pain magically disappear, nor does it protect you from ever getting hurt again. Healing provides a philosophy and a framework to process your experiences. It allows you to bring love to every situation; it empowers you to tap into your inner guidance and insert boundaries where needed. Those may seem like simple changes, but they can transform your life.

It's amazing how your priorities change when you are committed to your self-care and growth. You become your own best friend, and you respect the role of the Universe. If you speak to somebody who is committed to their healing, you will notice two things. They are very intentional, and they leave space for love and miracles to happen.

Healing may not be the easiest thing you do, but it will be gratifying. There's something so blissful and rewarding about reclaiming yourself. Somewhere along the line, you might have lost your voice, given up your power, or compromised your physical and emotional well-being. You might have abandoned your faith or values, but everything is right there for you to take back.

Here's what so many people forget. We all came into this world with a beautiful life force that is composed of God's unconditional love. That gives us purpose and value, and it never goes away no matter what we do. Now, we may experience a loss of confidence or low self-esteem, but that's different because we are measuring ourselves based on the world's superficial criteria for success and lovability … looks, performance, popularity, or material things.

Here's a better explanation. Your self-worth is unshakable because your value comes from within. It's not an external component. When you align with your heart and self-worth, you will find the quality of your life will go up. You start asking for more from yourself and the Universe because you believe that you are deserving.

We are vessels of energy, and when we show equal respect to pain as we do for love, we shall expand in glorious ways. Pain is here to teach you something. If you allow yourself to be with it long enough, it will direct you toward something liberating. Your inner guidance will inform you what that freedom is. It's likely to tie into some unexpressed desire that has been stirring for a very long time. It could be a healthier lifestyle, a supportive relationship, a new passion, or a stronger mindset.

Transformation happens when you meet your faith and vulnerability and uncover something incredible about yourself. However, if you resist the process and stay safe and insulated, you will miss the opportunity to expand. It would be like a caterpillar that never leaves its musty cocoon to take flight and show the world its beautiful wings.

During the early stages of writing this book, I told myself I wanted to help people feel better about themselves. However, during this process, I had to reevaluate that expectation. Where does that need for validation come from? What is it about my family history or upbringing that I thought I had to make others feel better? It forced me to dive much deeper into my story and my healing.

When I look back at my life, nobody assigned me the job of caretaker. It was just my way of adapting to energies in my home and the world. Now, I may not have been able to articulate it way back then, but I can see that my search for Grace actually started as a little girl. I wanted stability and safety for myself. I wanted to know self-love and how to bring in calm energy when my external world felt chaotic.

Survival behaviors don't just pop up out of the blue, and they don't just go away by themselves, either. You must advocate for yourself. It may require a few new tools, a support system, and an advanced philosophy to break through all the protective layers.

For me, that meant studying spirituality, becoming a Mind-Body Medicine Practitioner, and writing this book. It helped me unravel my story of codependency.

I had to dissect my role in my family and how that played out in my life. How did my emotional habits affect my self-esteem, choices, and relationships? I used this opportunity to ask myself for compassion and forgiveness. This process helped me untangle my story, process old hurts, arrive at self-love, and find my gratitude for each person who had an impact on my growth.

Here's what I now understand. When you're ready to go deeper into your story, the Universe will guide you through the process. There's nothing that needs to be fixed at this particular time. It's about coming to terms with your truth and acknowledging your family history and where you came from. After all, it has shaped you into the person that you are today.

You might find that some dysfunctional patterns in your family trace back several generations. Let that remind you of how brave you are right now to confront generational pain and heal those old wounds. I want to remind you that healing is not about rewriting history, rehashing pain, or bad-mouthing any person from your life. It's about coming to a deeper understanding of yourself and arriving back to unconditional love.

Here are some of the tools that you now have available to you.

Soft belly breathing can help calm your nervous system down when you're upset or stressed out.

Journaling will help you process your traumas or grief from a long time ago.

Meditations can help you navigate through emotional problems, difficult decisions, or serious health issues.

Movement will free your mind and body of tension and energetic blockages in your chakras.

Affirmations will restore your confidence and love for yourself.

At this stage, I've decided it's best to stay focused on the Grace that lives inside me. My worth cannot be attached to another person, but I do consult with my God on a regular basis. After years of writing and self-reflection, I've decided that I'm the only one who can heal me, and you are the only one who can heal you. However, should we affect one another in some beautiful way, then that is an honor for both of us.

Every chapter in this book has some unique perspective about love. I used to think that life was a **"luck thing."** You either have a good hand or a bad hand. Today I understand that all of our experiences are just extensions of the way we love ourselves. If you feel grief, stress, guilt, resentment or worry, then your experiences will project those negative energies. If you feel joyful, grateful, spiritual, and compassionate, you will cultivate massive love, connection, abundance, and joy.

If you're looking at your life right now and wondering why your body can't keep up, why people keep disappointing you, why you're stressed out or tired all the time, or why you feel like you're always swimming upstream, I encourage you to sit down at the kitchen table and pull out a chair. Allow your pain to have a seat at the table. Then, ask it what it wants you to know.

Believe it or not, it's our emotional habits that pose the greatest risk to our health because we can hide our pain and emotions for a long time. In fact, survival habits may go unnoticed indefinitely unless there's a crisis, a breakdown, a health problem, or a conflict that breaks the silence.

It may be a lot to unpack all at once, but once you apply these tools to your life, you're going to see amazing changes in yourself. You will start focusing on all the goodness around you instead of the limitations. That shift is incredible because you recognize that you belong here and your life has profound meaning.

The concept of wanting more doesn't necessarily mean that you're dissatisfied with yourself. It may, in fact, represent some larger commitment to love yourself and God. You are just acknowledging to yourself that you have more room to grow, and I encourage you to show off your amazing wings to the entire world.

I want to share a conversation that I had with my son Frank when we were on a ten-hour drive home to Arizona. He said, "Mom, as you close your book, think about how you want people to feel. You've asked them to look at areas of their lives that are hard and uncomfortable, but now you must allow them to see some light within themselves. The truth is, you can fall in love with the growth process as much as you fall in love with anything else. It's just that we aren't taught to view life in this way. You can fall in love with getting better, being more equipped to deal with adversity, and seeing your life bear fruit after an intense comeback. It's that space where we get really excited about the future, and that's where we get the inspiration to help other people win."

I felt a tingle run down my back. I was so thankful for his insight. He has walked with me throughout this entire journey, cheering me on and helping me find the courage to keep going when I was stuck on chapters. He also knows what it's like to want more in a world that gets confused in its priorities. He reminded me on that trip why I've poured years of my life into this book, and why I'm helping people reconnect with their dreams.

When you know your worth, you understand your "WHY" for being. This gives you the clarity to know what you are **"FOR"** instead of **"AGAINST."** This changes the chemistry in your body because you operate in abundance instead of resistance. This also makes a tremendous difference in manifesting powerful changes in yourself. It allows you to take all the extra weight off your shoulders, and it gives you the confidence to attract positive experiences and relationships. When you give yourself permission to heal, you essentially model courage and teach others to stand in the light where they can be seen and loved.

We have to let go of the guilt that it's okay to want more. Sometimes, we hold back from our abundance because we don't want to leave others behind. This happens frequently if there has been dysfunction or abuse in our family history. However, we cannot put limitations on our health and joy based on what others do or don't do ... even the people we love.

We need to stay in our lane. Sometimes our lane is faster, sometimes our lane is slower, but we cannot compare healing. People go deeper when they are ready and not a moment sooner. Your happiness and well-being cannot be contingent on whether you think others are okay. Once again, I bring you back to the mantra, **"Trust the Process."** Trust the timing of your life. After all, it is no coincidence that something brought you to this book at this particular time.

If something within you says:

"I'm tired of holding back ... "

"I'm tired of being stressed out and sick ... "

"I'm tired of watching life pass me by ... "

"I'm tired of going through the motions ... "

"I'm tired of holding everyone else's stuff ... "

Then guess what? **YOU DO WANT SOMETHING MORE,** and I want you to claim that for yourself.

It is now up to you to get clear on what it is in your life that requires your immediate attention and love. It wasn't that long ago that my dear friend Peach and I held a workshop on self-love. We asked the women to place their hands on their hearts, close their eyes, set aside their worries for a moment, and think about something they are inviting into their lives. Some struggled with the question, and others cried when they gave themselves permission to go there.

I actually had a brief moment of sadness too. I thought about how many of us postpone our happiness because we think we need to match the frequency of our family members, our friends, or the world. I'm here to remind you about the beautiful lotus that can bloom in the mud, and the dandelion that can grow through a crack in the sidewalk. You have that same resilience. You just need permission to love again and trust again. You, my friend, have a million dreams waiting for you. Take hold of every single one of them!

Stay in Purpose.

Love,

Krista

Exercise & Reflection

My friend Peach and I created this simple wheel to get you in touch with critical parts of your life that require attention and love. The wheel is broken down into 10 major pieces. This is a snapshot of life and where we are likely to pour our energy. I encourage you to reconstruct the circle in your journal so that you can keep a clean copy. Should you feel the need to add another category that represents your priorities, then just draw it in.

Ingredients for a Balanced Life

Part 1: Take a moment to look at each piece of pie and then use the friendly emoji faces to indicate where you currently stand with that category (thriving, so-so, or needs attention). Stay light. The whole reason for using emojis is to release the temptation to judge yourself.

Now, pull out your journal and answer the following questions:

Part 2: Look at the specific areas of your life that you are thriving in and give yourself kudos. Now, create a list of people and experiences that are presently supporting you. Write down as much as you can think of. This is a very healthy exercise to do on a regular basis because it allows you to see that you are being supported in a lot of places in your life. The positivity that you draw from your list feeds your spirit. It invokes higher vibrational emotions like love, gratitude, and joy. The more you affirm this energy in yourself, the more abundance you attract.

Part 3: Now, take a look at the areas of the pie that you selected that came up as "So-So" or "Needs TLC." List each one on your journal page and ask yourself how the phrase *"I want something more"* fits into this category. If you are unsure, skip it and come back to it at a later time. The most important part of this exercise is to acknowledge some part of your life that needs your love, understanding, and attention. This exercise could highlight the need for self-care, a date night, an exercise routine, financial management, self-reflection, family time, reconnecting with an old friend, energy clearing, or purging things in your home that no longer serve you.

Chapter Twenty-Three

The Field of Dreams

It's amazing what happens when you stay on top of self-care and manage your emotional needs. You have more freedom. You find more time to explore and play. So, where does all this new energy come from? Well, it's not that there's more hours in the day. You just become more conscious of your boundaries and more selective about where you place your time and energy.

Imagine that for a moment. What would it be like for you to do more of what you love? What would it be like to let go of doing things out of guilt or obligation? What would it be like to have somebody pull all that weight off your shoulders? Well, that someone is you! I promise you that everything gets better and lighter when you shift your attention inward.

It's ironic that most of us would drop everything to support a friend going through a difficult time. We would show them just how resilient they are and advise them to be patient with themselves. It's true that most of us have a secret code in which we show up for our friends with no questions asked. Then why is it that we lack that same compassion for ourselves? Are there different rules, and if so, what are they?

As long as we keep telling ourselves that we aren't good enough, committed enough, smart enough, or deserving, we are essentially putting up barriers for the Universe and others to support us. There is a tremendous cost to fear that nobody is talking about.

We lose ourselves, and we stop caring for our needs.

Whether we realize it or not, the Universe is generous and will provide support to you without doing a single thing, but it's your devotion to yourself and your spirituality that turns up the miracles in your life. Once you recognize your value, you no longer see yourself as separate from the divine—and guess what? You start showing up for yourself in the same way that you would do so for your best friend.

The Universe is an omnipresent energy that is on standby. You just have to tap in and ask for support. Think of that "I AM" energy that understands your needs at all times. When you become intentional about staying in this higher vibration, new doors open all the time, and you experience more synchronicities and blessings.

Look around your life. You don't have to be a psychologist to see who's operating at a high vibration and who is struggling. That's because we all feed off one another's energy. You can feel the difference between the person who is vibing with life. They are vibrant, passionate, and extremely grateful. They illuminate joy and light. Then there are the people who operate from a lower vibration. They struggle all the time. If you ask them, they tend to complain that they are depressed and overburdened, and they are often the victim in their story.

According to Abraham Hicks, each feeling holds a certain vibration. These feelings serve as a barometer for measuring frequency. She created **"The Emotional Guidance Scale,"** which lists 22 different emotions, with JOY being the highest and powerlessness being the lowest. This list could be life-changing for you because if you honestly ask yourself where you stand with your emotions, you can get a good read on your overall health, happiness, and attitude.

HERE IS THE LIST:

1) Joy/Knowledge/Empowerment/Freedom/Love/Appreciation

2) Passion

3) Enthusiasm

4) Positive Expectation/Belief

5) Optimism

6) Hopefulness

7) Contentment

8) Boredom

9) Pessimism

10) Frustration/Irritation/Impatience

11) Overwhelm

12) Disappointment

13) Doubt

14) Worry

15) Blame

16) Discouragement

17) Anger

18) Revenge

19) Hatred/Rage

20) Jealousy

21) Insecurity/Guilt/Unworthiness

22) Fear/Grief/Depression/Despair/Powerlessness[22]

I want you to notice that **"FEAR"** is at the very bottom. Right now, our entire world is holding onto fear. This isn't in the least bit surprising. This list is not only helpful in determining where your mindset is at, but it's also very helpful in understanding other people. It gives you some deeper insight and empathy.

Consider for a moment the woman who hasn't allowed herself to fully grieve the loss of her husband, the coworker who is underappreciated and overwhelmed with responsibilities, or the person who has allowed the fear of Covid to control their decisions. These lovely people don't realize how their lower frequency affects their mood, decisions, immunity, and relationships, not to mention their overall receptivity to receive support from the Universe.

If you want to improve any part of your life, then it will require you to raise your frequency. We've highlighted the benefits of maintaining a higher vibration. You feel lighter, open the portal to receive support, guidance, and messages from the other side, become emotionally, physically, and mentally stronger, and your

---

[22] Angie Swartz, "Abraham Hicks Emotional Guidance Scale and How to Use It," LIFE PUR-POSE ADVISOR, June 3, 2021, https://lifepurposeadvisor.com/abraham-hicks-emotional-guidance-scale-and-how-to-use-it/#:~:text=According%20to%20Abra-ham%20Hicks%2C%20your,and%20powerlessness%20(the%20lowest).

immunity increases. This also feeds right into the law of attraction. You attract what you focus on.

You can join forces with the Universe to elevate yourself and spread more love in the world. It's fascinating how it works. When you announce your vision, you activate an energy field that holds a place for you and the Universe to collaborate. I think of this shared space as a **"Field of Dreams."** It is where your higher self can take you to the next level of abundance. It's where dreams are born, and miracles are realized.

In the last chapter, I invited you to work with the wheel **(Ingredients for a Balanced Life).** You evaluated the different categories and decided which areas of your life need more attention and TLC. What if I told you that the Universe is waiting for you to share your desires so that you can experience more Grace & Ease?

I'm sure you have heard of the word **"manifest."** The simplest way to understand it is to recognize that human beings can bring emotions or something theoretical to reality. We can present the Universe with an idea, desire, or prayer to work on together. Say what you will, but there is something within all of us that is magical. When we align our energy and intentions with the spiritual realm, extraordinary things do happen.

In my home I have a quote hanging in my living room by Roald Dahl. It says, **"And above all, watch with glittering eyes the whole world around you because the greatest secrets are always hidden in the most likely places ... those who don't believe in magic will never find it."** It's true you can influence your health, relationships, career, and well-being by taking stock of your life and offering your intentions to the Universe.

God will play a prominent role in your dreams, but you need to get comfortable with one thing first: **"You must believe that you** are worthy to receive." It is estimated that human beings have about 60,000–80,000 thoughts per day. Have you ever asked yourself what is the tone of your inner dialogue? Do you lean toward positive or negative thoughts? Is the glass half full or half empty?

Should you be the person who manages your emotions regularly and participates in rituals of self-love and healing, then you are likely to have positive thoughts. If you are the person who regularly absorbs stress and fear and takes a defensive position on everything, then you are likely to generate negative thoughts. In this case, you cannot tap into your magnetic energy. It's a simple equation. We attract what we believe about ourselves. The survivalist who operates on fear and lack struggles with this concept because they don't feel worthy of love or goodness.

Of course, none of this information is new, but it's life-changing for the person who keeps wondering why they can't get ahead, why they can't pull themselves out of a toxic mindset, or why they feel stuck and all alone. Your emotions reflect your thoughts, beliefs, and self-talk, so the question to ask yourself right now is, **"What am I telling myself day in and day out?"** You can either talk yourself into your abundance or out of your abundance.

Here are some examples of heavier emotions and the thought patterns behind them:

If you feel afraid ... it's likely you have the belief that you aren't safe or protected.

If you feel unsuccessful ... it's likely you have the belief that you aren't good enough.

If you feel lonely ... it's likely you have the belief that you're not worthy of love.

If you feel jealous ... it's likely you have the belief that you don't have enough.

If you feel angry ... It's likely you have the belief that people are out to hurt you.

You can see through these examples that there is a cause and effect to everything. The mind-body spiritual connection is so strong that your thoughts can dictate an experience in your body and influence every area of your life. The more you study your thought patterns, the easier it is to shift habits that sabotage your happiness and well-being. Self-awareness builds confidence and reinforces positive energy.

So, let's talk about how you can use your thoughts for something good and how you can change any experience in your life for the better. I want to start with something playful. I invite you to pull out your journal and find a blank page. Write down the following: **"Wouldn't it be nice if ..."** Then have at it. Fill up your entire page with magical thoughts. Once you're done, write the word **"Wish List"** at the very top.

There is nothing too small or trivial to put on your wish list. Maybe it would be nice if someone brought you coffee every morning in bed, or you could have a healthy home-cooked meal every night. Maybe you've always wanted a garden. When it comes to this process, there is nothing too big. Perhaps you're ready to invite a partner into your life, land that ideal career position, or maybe you wish our country could find some common ground.

This process gives you permission to tap into your imagination, and there are no limitations to what is possible. This exercise is so playful and free-flowing. Now, here's one piece of important advice when it comes to manifesting. You cannot manifest from a place of lack, fear, desperation, or unworthiness. It doesn't work.

The Universe collaborates with us when we affirm love for ourselves, and we pair our intentions with something kind, altruistic, and heart-centered. For that reason, you must remain positive. If you allow self-judgment or criticism to come through, it negates the entire process.

The inner critic will tell you all the reasons why you DON'T deserve something good. **"You can't have that job because you're not smart enough! You can't have that relationship because you're not lovable! You can't have that larger house because you're not worthy!"** Time and time again, we sabotage our happiness and fulfillment by injecting fear and self-deprecating thoughts into our energy field. The best way to describe this is to compare it to a hostile working environment. The Universe needs a positive working environment.

To help you digest this information, I will share different recommendations to help you manifest your intentions. I have summed up the advice in **"5 Core Strategies for Manifesting."** They will help you create the ideal environment for your dreams.

How to Manifest/Core Strategy # 1

Silence that inner critic who tells you that you can't be happy, healthy, and loved. You must believe that you are worthy of goodness, opportunities, and abundance flowing to you and through you.

Next, avoid people and external influences that bring your frequency down. These disruptors interfere with the flow of blessings and opportunities that come your way. This is why it's important to evaluate your environment and circle of influence. Do you remember that old saying, **"You are who you hang out**

with?" You must be careful of who or what you allow into your mind because it takes just one negative thought to screw up the entire field.

What is a disruptor? It can refer to a person, place, or thing that interrupts a process, idea, or activity. It creates emotional barriers and energetic obstructions. Its presence can alter a person's thoughts, state of mind, behavior, and even nervous system. Here are some examples of disruptors. It may surprise you to learn that your environment and primary circle of influence may be holding you back.

Disruptors: Societal rules ~ cultural obligations ~ unhealthy family systems ~ news ~ politics ~ marketing ~ dysfunctional relationships ~ negative people who complain and gossip ~ narcissists ~ survival behaviors ~ perfectionism ~ trauma ~ grief ~ any sneaky beliefs that reinforce lack and tell you that you are not worthy or deserving

How to Manifest/Core Strategy # 2

Be open to receiving your blessings. It is important to align yourself with the frequency of what you are inviting into your life. Avoid disruptors and be careful of cross-messaging: saying one thing and contradicting yourself with conflicting actions.

When you set an intention and invite the Universe to participate in your dreams, you essentially open the door to all of your spiritual support. It is a collaboration like no other where you can call upon God, angels, guides, and your loved ones who have departed. Stepping into this role of co-creator ignites fire, passion, and enthusiasm, and you can expand your gifts in ways that you never thought were possible.

How to Manifest/Core Strategy # 3

See yourself in collaboration with the spiritual realm. You may invoke the love of your higher power, guardian angels, archangels, guides, and loved ones who have passed on. Believe that all are unified and actively supporting your highest good.

It's important to decide what you want and consider how that change can make you a better person. Pay attention to how you frame your intentions and desires. Keep in mind that the Universe operates in positives. If someone says out loud that they don't want to be sick, broke, tired, alone, unhappy, overweight, etc., then the brain hears the last thing stated, and registers the negative experience. Some people may not even realize that they are reinforcing lack, sickness, heaviness, exhaustion, and depression by the way that they communicate.

How to Manifest/Core Strategy # 4

State your intentions with love and positivity. The likelihood of manifesting what you want goes up exponentially when you affirm what you want in a positive way. It's also powerful to leave open space for the Universe to participate in ways that you never thought were possible.

Lastly, the most powerful approach to manifesting is stating your intentions as if they have already happened. Instead of saying, **"I hope to feel better,"** it would be more potent to say, **"I AM feeling strong and healthy in my body."** This leaves no confusion.

Here's another example, **"I am trying to find a life partner"** can be framed with certainty and emotion. **"I AM so excited that I have met an incredible man who treats me with respect and affection. We are having the best time together!"**

The more specific you are with the Universe, the better your chances are to meet your desires. When you give all the delicious details about what the experience will look and feel like, then the Universe has very little interpretation to do. This is why people cut out pictures and powerful words and create vision boards. They write out their goals and dreams and make copies for various places in their home environment. When you get your five senses involved, you elevate the probability that your wish will come true.

How to Manifest/Core Strategy # 5

Be specific with what you are manifesting. Use descriptions of how you want the experience to feel. Write out your vision as if it has already happened. "I AM" is a wonderful way to frame your goal and stay in a higher frequency. Read your goal out loud daily and share it with others so that they may also hold the vision for you. Repeat the process as needed to make any alterations that meet your needs.

The human body is composed of matter and energy. Therefore, there is an energetic response to everything that you put out to the world ... your love, good thoughts, random acts of kindness, and your intentions. When you pair this goodness with the Universe, a divine orchestration starts happening behind the scenes. It's unimaginable to most human beings because we have been conditioned to be realists. We want proof, but faith requires trust and belief in something that is not visible.

For most of us, we might play along with the idea that wishes can come true. We may look for falling stars with our children, blow dandelion seeds off a little flower, or indulge a crowd at a party by closing our eyes and pausing just before we blow out our birthday candles. So, here's a question to consider: do you actually believe that your wishes can come true?

Don't answer that yet. This chapter may, in fact, be the most powerful one yet because it's nudging you to connect with your inner child, who is magical, and a Universe that is powerful beyond measure. You see, once God gets hold of your dreams, they get bigger because they take on mass and kinetic energy. Things start falling into place in the most surprising ways. It's because it's no longer a quiet little secret or half-assed dream. It becomes a shared miracle.

Nothing happens without your intention and some action to back it up. This is true of every aspect of your life: your family, health, career, education, partnership, creativity, friendships, spiritual growth, and financial abundance. The fact that you have a force field to tap into is absolutely incredible. Leave nothing to chance. If you care about it, decide what you want, carve out an intention, and share it with the Universe as soon as possible. I promise it is you who will have the glittering eyes.

Stay in the Flow.

Love,

Krista

Exercise & Reflection

Part 1: Take a look at the list from **"The Emotional Guidance Scale."** Ask yourself what words currently describe your mood. Once you get an honest read, ask yourself if there is anything that you can do right now to elevate your frequency. Take a moment to write down some activities that you enjoy that can help you shift your energy and attitude.

Here are some additional suggestions: Spend time in nature, do soft belly breathing, listen to a meditation, shake and dance, take a hot shower, hydrate, have a nutritious meal, call a friend, exercise, go for a walk, take a hot shower, listen to music, take a nap, write in your journal, spend time in the garden, or color.

Part 2: It's time to play with the Universe. Select one entry from the **"Wish List"** that you wrote out earlier in the chapter. For example, if you selected, "Wouldn't it be nice if I found my dream job," reframe the wish into stronger statements that inform the Universe what you desire. Remember, it's much more powerful to be as specific as possible. Elaborate on what the job looks and feels like. Add any additional details that you think are important. Before you close your statement, let the Universe know that you seek this vision or something more grand to support your highest good. This tells the Universe that you are open to receiving and not attached to just one outcome.

Here is an example. **"I AM so excited that I am working at my dream job as an English teacher at Boulder Creek High School. This job is rewarding, and I'm thrilled to be working with the Senior Class. I am so grateful that I found a job that is close to my home, the salary meets all my needs, and the schedule works with my children's daycare hours. I ask the Universe for**

**support for this vision or something better. I am open to re-
ceive what is in the highest good for myself and for all concerned."** Be sure to frame your intention in such a way that it's
already in your field and making a difference.

When you are done, make several copies and place them in areas
of your environment that have your energy. You might want to
put one on your nightstand, in your car, or by your favorite reading chair. Make it a habit to read your intentions out loud daily.
You may want to share it with another person so that they hold
your vision as well. Have fun!

Chapter Twenty-Four

Starting Over

And so here we are … the very last chapter! If it's possible to feel excitement and melancholy all at once, that's where my emotions are right now. I'm proud of the work that went into this book. I can remember trying to come up with a title. I wanted something that would bring self-kindness and resilience to the forefront, and so I chose *The Search for Grace … Heal Your Life From the Inside Out.*

My studies in Mind-Body Medicine and Spirituality greatly contributed to the content of the book, but it was my life experiences that became the heart of the chapters. Looking back, from the moment I arrived on this earth, I have been learning how to love and how to let go. For years, I have been searching for balance between my inner self and the outer world. I've also had to meet more personal challenges with codependency and perfectionism.

All of that emotional work required a certain amount of time and perseverance, and that's why I can say with great pride that my research for this book began long before I ever became an author. Since I was a little girl I have been learning to live comfortably in my skin and stand in my story without shame or apology.

As a grown woman, I have been confronting things in myself that aren't particularly flattering, and here's what I've learned. Every person has faults and embarrassing things tucked away in their past, and there isn't a single family on this planet that doesn't have flaws and problems. I suppose this is why the human experience is considered a spiritual journey. It's taking us to another place ... another state of mind and consciousness.

When you stop hiding your emotions, your grief, and painful things from your past, you liberate yourself from fear and open your heart to a world of wonder. Standing in your truth has to be one of the most powerful things you can do for yourself, but it doesn't just benefit you. It helps your family, your circle of friends, your community, and the next generation. Here's an interesting fact. If trauma isn't healed, it will pass through several generations until someone is brave enough to confront it.

It's true; the best part of life is building relationships and allowing another human being to see your heart up close. However, it's also the trickiest part about life too because you risk getting hurt. It's a dynamic that is glorious one moment and painstaking the next. Here's the greater point ... your relationships are teaching you how to be more compassionate. They're showing you how to value yourself and appreciate the nuances of life.

If you think about it, nothing in this life belongs to us, including our relationships. The only exception to that is the relationship that we have with ourselves and God. As far as we know, enlightenment is the gentlest path to peace and harmony. It shouldn't surprise anyone that the person who consistently works on themselves doesn't have time for gossip or criticism. They are too busy creating a meaningful legacy. That's what self-discovery does. It allows you to meet your greatest potential to give love and receive love.

Of course, understanding yourself doesn't happen overnight or without mistakes. There have been plenty of moments where I have felt **"graceless,"** and I've run myself down to keep up with the appearance that I had my shit together. We are going to stumble from time to time, and we are all going to question whether we are on the right path. Just remember that it's a process, and there are no timelines. As long as you are here, you have the opportunity to expand.

I took on this spiritual assignment of writing this book with the hope that I could make a difference and become a better person through the process. At times, it was frustrating, and I wanted to give up. I fought myself more than I wanted to, but there was something inside me that knew this book must take flight.

This process has shown me that nothing positive happens without our intention and participation. You are the only one who can make joy sustainable. It's YOUR decision to heal, embrace your story, use your gifts, and get healthier. You're the only one who can decide how deep you want to go in your relationships. I would be lying if I said it was easy, but it's amazing how support shows up when you are doing something brave. The Universe responds to your courage.

I have often wondered, **"What if every single turn in my life brought me to this moment? What if the very same things that seemed to break my heart and my spirit were the same things that gave me purpose?"** It's funny how spirituality gives you an entirely different perspective. When you're in the muck, it's painful. The last thing you want to believe is that there's purpose in grief, trauma, sickness, or turmoil. However, if you trust that God has something powerful for you to do in this lifetime, you will see that you are invited to be a conduit for love.

In the end, I know that these chapters can support you. They can help you break down emotional barriers, dismantle belief systems that reinforce fear, and pull back the curtain on survival behaviors that keep you in a state of stress, lack, or unworthiness.

Whether it's the role of family systems, social conditioning, news, media, marketing, or politics, you now have the tools to recognize fear. These influences are competing for your time, energy, and allegiance. If you aren't self-aware or paying attention, then you will lose yourself to all the stress, social pressure, and negativity. They may try to dictate your decisions and habits, but you get to decide whether you will listen to your heart or to the noise.

Remember, you have absolute free will to decide your path at all times. You get to turn things on and off. This is why it's good to pull over, step away from the noise, and get your bearings. It helps you collect your thoughts, weed out superficial relationships and soulless causes, and observe where all your energy is going. It also allows you to check in with your body and your emotions. Your intuition will always alert you if something doesn't feel right.

Reflection is a big part of your emotional maintenance.

Should you wonder where to start, you can begin with these questions:

1) Does my current routine, environment, relationships, and mindset support my well-being?

2) Am I coming from a state of love or a state of fear right now?

3) Is there any person or source causing me stress at this particular time?

4) Does my body have a message for me?

5) Can I take a little time away from my busy life to connect with my higher self?

These regular **"check-ins"** have been life-changing. They've helped me instill self-care, administer pep talks, and release the things that don't serve my highest good. I've started treating my-self more like a close friend, and that's something new for me.

As I look back at this entire journey, I can see that everything had divine timing. I say that not because it was perfect but because I was channeling my intuition and higher guidance all the time. It was powerful how the chapters started writing themselves. I would often step back after an intense writing session and say, **"How did I know that?"** There were many times when I may have typed on the keyboard, but God told me what to write.

I take a lot of pride in knowing that my journey looks a lot like yours. It's not that we have parallel lives; it's that we have both experienced the deepest love, and we have suffered some of the most heart-wrenching losses. That is our universal experience. Life has peaks and valleys and wins and losses, and it's up to us to learn how to make those transitions as smooth as possible.

Whether you realize it or not, love or fear can become a habit. Just remember that love comes from a higher frequency, and it will propel you forward. Fear, on the other hand, has a density about it and stalls everything: healing, transformation, and social progress. Fear can be so paralyzing that people lose track of their priorities. With every shakedown, you will be humbled, and your higher self will ask you to make a decision, **"Are you going to hold onto faith or fear?"**

All those adversities that you have gone through in your life have exposed some rather harsh realities of the world and the human condition. However, every moment of human frailty, every crisis, loss, dysfunctional relationship, or disaster has helped you clarify what really matters to you. If you can remember that every obsta-cle that passes through your life has the potential to become a

"Love Story," then you won't find yourself on an emotional rollercoaster all the time. No matter what the situation is, it's teaching you to **LOVE SOMETHING** ... love yourself, love God, love your country, or love another person.

While society continues to promote superficial rewards, we can select a path of substance. The distractions and short-term gratifications are masquerading as happiness, but none of it is sustainable. Life is about the renovation of self, the glorious exchange between human beings, the long path home, and creating everlasting peace.

One of the most important things to remember about your healing is that you never stay in one place for too long. The truth is that you have to be able to reference joy and pain to expand your consciousness. One cannot be happy 24/7, nor can we insulate ourselves from pain. If you look deeper into the human condition, you shall see that all life experiences, regardless of their label **"good or bad,"** are just redirecting you back to the same place ... your faith.

So many people can't be bothered with God, and they want little to do with healing, and yet it is the greatest reason for our suffering in today's world. People are willing to bankrupt their checking accounts and their souls just to keep up with a chaotic world. However, what they are also finding is that it's a very lonely existence. Spirituality is a **"CROSS ROAD."** I mean that literally and figuratively. You are invited to see yourself in spiritual development.

Spirituality remains one of the greatest support systems available to us and yet there's a huge campaign against it in today's world. Hopefully, this book has challenged you to ask yourself why that is. Spirituality is about holding ourselves to a higher level of morality, consciousness, and love. Because it questions the motives and integrity of people in power, there is great resistance.

When you know this, you become more selective about who you follow, what you watch, and where you place your energy.

My mother-in-law Cathy used to say, **"If God takes you to it ... then he will take you through it."** You might have a ton of reasons why you avoid pain and hold everything inside. It may trace back to your childhood. Maybe you kept the peace in your family; maybe you felt like you needed to establish safety or protection; maybe you had no other alternative. The challenge with that behavior is that your body can't keep up, and the charade gets old. Something vital in your life will eventually break down, and so I say this to you, **"You are not bound to pain, and you are not bound to anything in your life that no longer serves your highest good. It's absolutely okay to start over."**

I remember the day my husband and I rolled the moving truck out of my driveway. I saw my whole life flash before my eyes. I saw myself as a little girl playing jacks in my room, I saw myself as a raging teenager smoking and drinking and desperate for attention, I saw myself as a hopeful bride on my wedding day, I saw a new home being built in Petaluma, I remember what it was like when the nurse laid my sons on my chest for the first time, I remember my boys playing basketball in the driveway, I saw birthday celebrations, block parties, and funerals. Something told me that every stage was necessary for my growth, and a voice told me, **"It's going to be okay."**

I didn't know that stepping away from everything that felt safe and comfortable would somehow make me stronger ... but it did. It's true that human beings don't like to change very much. Perhaps it's because we can't be very good at it because we're stepping into the unknown. Sometimes we hold onto things out of habit or fear even when something has proved to be unhealthy or we have outgrown a situation. My hope is that you look back on this time with me and remember that life has lots of chapters, and you will start over many times.

I used to think it would have been nice to have all these tools and wisdom when I was that little girl, but I now see that it would have changed everything. I wouldn't be the person that I am to-day. I have a beautiful life, and it's because of ALL the things I went through, ALL the things I fought for, and ALL the pain that I had the courage to heal.

When I wrote the tagline, **"Heal Your Life From the Inside Out,"** I wanted you to know that peace is an inside job. So many people want to bypass the spiritual work and seek some quick fix, but it doesn't work that way. In order to heal, you must release the judgments and expectations of others and become your own advocate. That means that you give yourself permission to feel everything, express your emotions and your needs, and cry if you must.

The process of letting go doesn't have to be devastating, particu-larly if you are ready to invite positive energy into your life. You are stronger for everything you have gone through, not because you handled life perfectly but because your life experiences have given you the gift of knowing yourself and God on a much deeper level.

I want to come back to the word **"GRACE,"** which may have felt a bit elusive up until now. Finding Grace is not about reaching a particular place or destination. It simply means that you arrive back to your true self and you can love yourself unconditionally. Most importantly, you are willing to claim your divinity, that part of yourself that is synonymous with God.

On the morning that I was finishing up the last chapter of this book, Paul and I took the dog out for our usual walk. It was the same dirt path that we take every day. However, on this particular morning, it felt very different ... I felt different. I announced to him that after years of writing, **"I finished up my book."** I also confessed that I felt very emotional. You see, it was no longer some far-fetched dream, and it was no longer some ridiculous assignment I had given myself years ago. This book is now a shared miracle among every person I have loved and learned from. Most importantly, it had Cathy's love.

As we walked on that trail, I saw the most spectacular sign. There were dragonflies everywhere. That may not seem like a big deal, but sighting a single dragonfly has always given me goosebumps because it reminds me of Cathy. Today, there were about twenty of them dancing across the sky. Some were red and others were shades of blue and green. I wondered if it was a fluke of some sort or if it was a sign from God telling me, **"I knew you could do it!"**

They say that a dragonfly is a symbol of transformation, and I feel like a changed woman. I am no longer chasing Grace. I now see it as an extension of myself. This book was my journey to become a better person, not just for myself but for my parents, my siblings, my husband, my sons, and my dog. I want every generation before me and after me to know that pain has a gift, and we need to embrace our healing.

I gave this book everything. It's true that not everybody understood it, but I did ... and so did God. As I sit and reflect on this entire process, I'm reminded of a conversation I had with my Cousin Benny, who welcomed me to Arizona. **"You came here to find out who you really are as a teacher. You may have thought that you gave up everything to start over, but like the story of the Phoenix, it is about the rising, the rebirth, and the regeneration."**

I'll never forget his words because there was something inside me that believed that I was meant to soar. I always knew that my story was taking me to another level. I just didn't know where or who I would affect along the way. The truth is, we won't ever know our complete impact in this life, and this is yet another reason to be faithful. Collaborations happen all the time between our higher selves. Ram Dass said it best with his metaphorical quote, **"We're all just walking each other home."**

Now, just because this book is done doesn't mean that my spiritual work ends. Somehow, it's all just getting started. In some glorious exchange of human energy, you and I were meant to come together on this journey, and I am grateful. I truly want the highest good for you, for me, and for humanity. It's that kindness and wholesome energy that we can build upon.

I talked about feeling different deep inside my soul. My prayer is that some part of you feels different too. Now that you have this new toolbox and a crazy positive attitude to fall back on, I suspect that you'll look at the world with a whole new lens. You see, everybody needs healing, and the sooner we normalize this conversation, the sooner we can get the world back on track. We must see that the turmoil we are experiencing as a society is just a symptom of emotional and spiritual neglect. **We need to be REAL again.**

Well, it was just twenty-four little chapters that I put together. No big deal, right? I'm laughing as I'm typing this because it was a huge fucking deal! My mind, body, and heart are finally on the same page, and it feels amazing. I hope that some part of you feels inspired to pull off to the side and unravel your own story. If you haven't figured it out by now, you are here by design. **You are part WARRIOR & MIRACLE!** Treat yourself with love, tend to your needs, and celebrate your progress as you go.

My guess is that you're going to do more of what makes you

happy, and stop postponing your joy. I'm so excited for you to honor yourself and nourish a life that fulfills you. Don't waste another minute subscribing to fear and holding yourself back to appease others. Oh ... and one last thing. Just remember that this book was never about changing who you are. It was about getting in touch with the REAL YOU and recognizing that Grace has been with you the entire time.

Stay Graceful.

Love,

Krista

I pondered whether I should include one final exercise or perhaps a final meditation. I asked God, **"How does this whole thing end?"** I sat with that question for several days. Eventually, I heard two words with rather profound instructions: **"Pace Yourself."**

I closed my eyes and allowed the words to pour through me. I wrote down each verse that I heard in my head. I knew that it was coming from a higher place. As you will see, it ties up our time together quite nicely. Once I finished writing the passage, I sat with it and read it over and over. I was enamored with the symbolism of the wolf and the tree. It felt like it was God's signature on the book. It was definitely some parting advice for you and me to stay humble and grounded while we are on this human journey.

Here you go ...

Pace Yourself

In a world that wants you to hurry up and buy into chaos …
pace yourself.

There's no rush and no hustle when you are aligned
with your heart.

You see, the world wants you to believe that you have not done
enough to earn your place.

"Hurry up!

You must do more!

You must have more!"

But that is the wolf inside you that is never satisfied.

Look around. The pack is always tired, angry, and hungry.

You must be willing to sit still. Find a tree and wrap your hands
around the trunk.

Go to that quiet place inside yourself that is soft and gentle
like a bird. Be weightless.

Let go of the snarls and fear that there isn't enough for you.

You were born from pure love and abundance.

The feeling of lack that exists comes from separation
and survival.

You may have grown up very quickly, but do not lose that part
of yourself that wants to play,

paint, and hold hands. People will pass you up, and that is okay.

"Just pace yourself, and you will find your own lane."

Be intentional with your energy. Rest and pray when
you need to. Sing when you want to.

Allow my light to shine through you so that love is effortless.

Do not carry the weight of anger, comparison, or regret.

Remember that you are your own healer.

Like the tree, there is grace and purpose within you, but you
must untangle yourself from the

wolf, which represents doubt and fear. Be brave enough to sit
with your true self.

Honor that part of you that has been broken into a thousand
pieces, and align yourself with that

place within that is wise, whole, and spiritual. Do not be concerned with people who appear to

have more, for they, too, have their struggles. The truth is
…when you go at your own pace and

honor your sacred path, you have everything you need.

And so it is …

Stay well, my friend.

About the Author

K rista Gawronski authored her first book, *Soul Purpose ... Find the Courage to Fly,* in February of 2015. It inspired readers to follow their inner calling. Krista shares her own story of starting a nonprofit and how charity can open the door to love, miracles, human connection, and a deeper purpose within. Her second book, *Be Good ... The Heart-Centered Journey,* came out in September of 2018. It has a timeless message about self-compassion and humanity. The book starts backward and represents the arduous journey to find a sense of home and belonging in oneself.

Krista's education and life experiences culminate beautifully in her new book, *The Search for Grace ... Heal Your Life From the Inside Out.* She teaches her reader to become their own healer and advocate. She highlights the importance of self-care and maintaining energy in today's fast-moving world. Krista invites the reader to **"Stay Real"** and connect with Grace to maintain a physical, emotional, psychological, and spiritual balance.

When Krista is not writing, she loves to spend time with her family and friends. She enjoys taking walks with her dog, Nala, and exploring the desert for heart-shaped rocks. She swears that Anthem sunsets are extra special at Joyce's Joint, and the margaritas are outstanding. She loves being a Rotarian and promoting service and good deeds. Her passion is facilitating wellness groups, organizing workshops for women, and speaking on topics that relate to wellness, the human condition, and spirituality. She considers her life a great love story because she gets to share it with her husband, Paul, and her two sons, Frank and Vince. Krista's mantra is simple, **"Live What You Love."**

Stay Connected

Connect with Krista Gawronski:
KristaGawronski.com

To contact Krista with questions or requests, please email:
info@KristaGawronski.com

Find her books on Amazon ~ Author Central
www.amazon.com/stores/Krista-Gawronski/
author/B0172JJMG4

Connect with Krista on Facebook:
Facebook.com/soulpurpose16

Connect on Instagram:
Instagram.com/Krista_Gawronski

To join her women's group (Desert Bloom) in Anthem:
Facebook.com/groups/desertbloom16